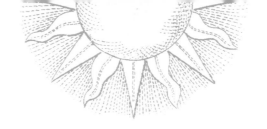

THE GREAT
HISPANIC HERITAGE

Pablo Picasso

THE GREAT HISPANIC HERITAGE

THE GREAT
HISPANIC HERITAGE

Pablo Picasso

Tim McNeese

CHELSEA HOUSE
PUBLISHERS

An imprint of Infobase Publishing

Pablo Picasso

Copyright © 2006 by Infobase Publishing

Chelsea House
An imprint of Infobase Publishing
132 West 31st Street
New York NY 10001

Library of Congress Cataloging-in-Publication Data

McNeese, Tim.
  Pablo Picasso / Tim McNeese.
     p. cm. — (Great Hispanic heritage)
  Includes bibliographical references and index.
  ISBN 0-7910-8843-X (hard cover)
  1. Picasso, Pablo, 1881-1973—Juvenile literature. 2. Artists—France—Biography—Juvenile literature. I. Title. II. Series.
  N6853.P5M353 2005
  709.2—dc22
                              2005025999

Series design by Terry Mallon
Cover design by Keith Trego

Printed in the United States of America

Bang EJB 10 9 8 7 6 5 4 3 2 1

This book is printed on acid-free paper.

All links and web addresses were checked and verified to be correct at the time of publication. Because of the dynamic nature of the web, some addresses and links may have changed since publication and may no longer be valid.

Table of Contents

1

On the Wings of Death

At 4:40 on the afternoon of April 26, 1937, shopkeepers, street vendors, and shoppers in the town of Guernica, Spain, were enjoying themselves. On that sunny Mediterranean afternoon, the town's streets were bustling. It was Monday—market day—in this otherwise quiet town, situated in northeastern Spain, in the Basque province of Vizcaya. The weekly shopping day usually brought 2,000 people into Guernica, swelling the town's population to 12,000.

Suddenly, the skies above the sleepy Basque town were filled with foreign aircraft. Military planes were not unknown to the Basques in the region. The Spanish Civil War was in its second year. The war had become intensely violent, pitting the forces of the Fascist general Francisco Franco against the Nationalist armies of the new but shaky Spanish republican government. The ruthless Franco was promising economic prosperity and political stability to the Spanish people. In the midst of civil war, though, his military strategy was about to deliver death by proxy.

Franco's battle to establish Fascism and topple the democratic government of Spain had gained the support of other Fascist leaders, including Adolf Hitler of Germany and Benito Mussolini of Italy. Hitler was assisting Franco by supplying him with the weaponry of war, including tanks and some of the newest planes emerging from German airplane factories. Before the Spanish Civil War came to an end in 1939, more than 20,000 uniformed Germans would see duty in Spain.

The commander of the Luftwaffe, the German air force, was Hermann Goering. He had decided to use the Spanish Civil War as an opportunity to test out some of these new planes, especially bombers. He chose the Condor Legion to lead the attack over Guernica. The Condor consisted of 100 planes and more than 5,000 men. Its commander was Wolfram von Richthofen, a cousin of Manfred von Richthofen, the Red Baron—the legendary German pilot of World War I. Von Richthofen was intent on establishing his own wartime legend, and his pilots were ready and eager to gain some experience carrying out the new German style of warfare—blitzkrieg, or lightning war—that would include swift and well-coordinated air and ground assaults. On this sunny, spring afternoon, the Nazi war machine would take a test run over Guernica.

Although Guernica was many miles from the front where Republican and Fascist forces were engaged, there was a local bridge near an important road junction that Franco's forces believed might be of use to the Republicans. The bridge became the immediate target of the attack. The bridge was not the only target of the Germans that fateful day, however. If Von Richthofen was only interested in knocking out the bridge, he would have sent Stuka dive bombers to carry out the singular mission. The Stukas each carried a single bomb weighing half a ton. The Stukas were fitted with the latest bombsights, and a single half-ton bomb would have destroyed the bridge.

The Germans were intent on more than just destroying a bridge. They intended to target the entire population of Guernica. To that end, General von Richthofen dispatched three types of German planes over the town, including Junkers and Heinkel bombers, as well as Heinkel fighters. The Heinkel He 111 bomber could travel more than 250 miles per hour, with a flying range of more than 1,200 miles. This deadly bomber carried more than 3,700 pounds of bombs, and it was armed with six machine guns. Some of these planes were equipped to carry a bomber load that included 3,000 two-pounder aluminum incendiary projectiles, designed to ignite on a target and burst into flames. Although the Basque fishing village had no military significance, the Germans had selected the city for no reason other than for target practice.

As Nazi planes swooped down on the unsuspecting civilians of Guernica, their pilots unleashed a continuous assault of bombs and machine gun fire that lasted for three hours. On the streets of Guernica, civilians scattered in panic, and bombs screamed down from the sky. Incendiary bombs engulfed whole blocks in flames, causing the ground temperature at street level to reach 3,000 degrees. Bodies were ignited, and, even after the attack was over, the stench of burned flesh filled the streets. Those not killed by bomb explosions and firebombs were targeted by pilots and shot down by machine gun fire.

Some terrorized civilians managed to escape the inferno of Guernica's buildings and streets, fleeing into the nearby farm fields. They, too, were targeted. Those who survived later described how German planes flew in over the fields so low that they could clearly describe the facial features of the pilots. Juan Silliaco was in the streets during the attack but survived. Later, he wrote of the horrors he witnessed that afternoon:

> The air was alive with the cries of the wounded. I saw a man crawling down the street, dragging his broken legs . . . Pieces of people and animals were lying everywhere . . . In the wreckage

On April 26, 1937, during the Spanish Civil War, the village of Guernica (pictured here) was bombed by the German Luftwaffe (air force). When Pablo Picasso heard of the news in Paris, he set out to depict the violence and chaos of that infamous day. In early July, he unveiled his powerful antiwar painting, which he titled *Guernica*.

there was a young woman. I could not take my eyes off her. Bones stuck through her dress. Her head twisted right around her neck. She lay, mouth open, her tongue hanging out. I vomited and lost consciousness.[1]

Death and destruction reigned over the innocent village of Guernica. The town's buildings were on fire and would burn for days to follow. During those bloody three hours, 1,850 people were killed.

At the end of the attack, the bridge outside the town, the alleged target of the Nazi bombers, was still intact. No planes had scored a direct hit on the bridge. As for General von Richthofen, he recorded in the pages of his personal diary the results of the "concentrated attack" against Guernica, noting that the assault "was a great success."[2]

AN OUTRAGED SPANIARD

As word of the atrocities the Nazis had committed at Guernica filtered out across Europe and beyond, millions of people were outraged. Three days after the attack, word reached Paris. On May 1, one million protesters filled the streets of the City of Light in an immense display of support for the Basque victims of Fascist aggression and in outraged protest toward Franco, Hitler, and his Nazi war machine. One resident of Paris was especially outraged by the brutal German attack—a Spanish painter who supported the Nationalist government against Franco: Pablo Picasso.

The bombing of the Spanish town of Guernica had been planned for months prior to its launch. During those same months in early 1937, Picasso had been planning a special art project. He had been asked to produce a mural for the Spanish Government Pavilion at the Paris International Exhibition. Since the work would cover a large space, Picasso needed a much larger work studio than usual. Fortunately, Dora Maar, his current love interest, knew of an immense, available room, which had been used most recently as a lecture hall by the poet Georges Bataille. (Dora was Bataille's former lover.) The room was on the second floor of a seventeenth-century manor house on the Rue des Grands-Augustins, in Paris, near the Seine River. Months went by before Picasso selected the subject for his grand mural. At one point, he planned a work depicting an artist painting in his studio from a life model, but he scrapped that idea. When his inspiration finally came to him, it arrived on the wings of death delivered by the German Luftwaffe.

Over the next 10 days, he created 25 sketches. On May 11, he set up the giant canvas on which he would paint his mural. It measured nearly 26 feet in length, stood 11-and-a-half-feet tall, and spanned a total of 312 square feet. His specially

Pablo Picasso, pictured here in 1935, created thousands of paintings, prints, illustrations, and sculptures. The prolific artist produced 45 preparatory sketches and seven outlines for *Guernica*, leading up to its final incarnation.

selected Parisian studio was lengthy enough to accommodate the long canvas, but the ceiling was too short. He had to place his canvas on a slant. To paint on the great surface, "he would climb up and down a ladder, moving it in short hauls the length of the room as he went; where the canvas slanted away from his reach he employed a special long-handled brush, leaning precariously forward from his ladder perch."[3]

Working quickly, under great emotion, Picasso wasted no time sketching the initial outline for his mural on the canvas. In all, he produced 45 preparatory sketches. He produced six outlines of the symbolic work until he created a seventh and final one. As he developed his angry work, Dora was almost constantly in the room, supporting her lover. She was a professional photographer, and she used her camera to document every step in the mural's creation, a series depicting all seven versions of the gigantic painting. Picasso worked and reworked his outlines over a three-week period. With the memory of the attack against Guernica still fresh in the minds of many, Picasso finished his grand painting by early June.

More than 70 years after its creation, Picasso's *Guernica* remains one of the most powerful antiwar works of modern art ever created. Yet the work does not show a single bomb, tank, or rifle. Only a few flames of destruction are visible at the top right of the immense work. Instead, Picasso chose not to display the machines or even men of war but the effects and aftermath. As one observer of the work noted: "*Guernica* is an unheard scream."[4]

2

The Artist as a Young Man

Pablo Picasso was born on October 25, 1881, in Malaga, a small city in Spain's Andalusia region, situated along the southern coast. The time was 11:15 P.M., but Picasso would later claim that his birth took place at the stroke of midnight. The day of the great artist's birth was nearly his last. He was delivered by a midwife, but he did not breathe and was declared stillborn. An uncle, Dr. Salvador Ruiz, was present in the room, though, and blew cigar smoke into the infant's nose, causing the baby to revive. In Picasso's words: "I made a face and began to cry."[5]

His parents came from minor aristocratic families. His father was Don José Ruiz y Blasco, a tall, red-headed man, himself an artist. To friends and family, Pablo Picasso's Spanish father was known as "The Englishman," partly because of his red hair and partly because he was a lifelong admirer of the British and their culture. Friends knew him to be a shy man but one with a sense of humor. Don José was a teacher in Malaga's San Telmo School of Fine Arts. He was also

Maria Picasso Lopez is depicted here in an 1896 pastel on paper portrait by her son. The daughter of a Spanish government bureaucrat, Maria married Don José Ruiz y Blasco in 1880, and Pablo was born the following year.

curator of a local art museum. His specialty was the middle-class paintings of the period, mostly landscapes and still lifes. As Picasso later recalled, his father's artistic creations were simple and commonplace; they included "dining room pictures, the kind with partridges and pigeons, hares and rabbits, fur and feather. Fowl and flowers. Especially pigeons and lilies."[6]

Young Picasso's mother was Maria Picasso Lopez, a small-framed, black-haired beauty, the daughter of a Spanish government bureaucrat who had disappeared while working in Cuba when Maria was very young. José married Maria against his family's wishes. Spanish custom dictated that the families of young men such as José chose their wives, and José refused to accept the bride his family selected, deciding stubbornly to marry instead the woman's cousin, Maria. As young Pablo grew up, he seemed to have inherited his father's stubborn streak.

When José and Maria married in 1880, he was 42 years old and she was only 25. Picasso always remembered his mother as an optimistic woman, ever cheerful and positive. She is described by one of Picasso's biographers as "vivacious, good-humored and incorrigibly optimistic."[7] As her son grew up and revealed an interest in art, she professed a great faith in young Pablo and his abilities as an artist. In Picasso's early years as a young adult who struggled to develop a career and name in the art world, Maria "offered him both moral and financial support and Pablo always had great affection for her."[8]

By early November, the new son of Maria and José was baptized in a church in the neighboring town of Santiago. Pablo's baptismal name was lengthy, the result of a Spanish custom that honored people special to the families of Maria and José—Pablo Diego José Francisco de Paula Juan Nepomuceno Maria de los Remedios Cipriano de la Santisima Trinidad Ruiz Picasso. When the young child grew up, he would sign his paintings with the name "P. Ruiz" or "P. Ruiz Picasso." By the time he turned 20, though, the name was whittled down even further to simply one word—Picasso.

The details of Picasso's early years are vague. The artist himself spoke little of his childhood, but some of his memories are vivid and rich. He remembered experiencing an earthquake when he was only three years old: "My mother wore a handkerchief on her head, I had never seen her like that before. My father seized his cape from the coat-stand, threw it round his shoulders, took me in his arms and rolled me in its folds, leaving only my head exposed."[9] While taking shelter in the house of a family friend during the earthquake, Maria gave birth to her second child, a baby girl named Lola. There were other memories, as well. Picasso recalled learning to walk "by pushing a tin of Olibet biscuits because I knew what was inside."[10]

According to Maria, the infant Picasso began drawing before he could even talk. She told a story about young Pablo and his first word—*piz*—which referred to *lapiz*, the Spanish

A BRIDE OF HIS CHOOSING

As an adult, Pablo Picasso noted the extraordinary love he felt for his mother, Maria Picasso Lopez, as he grew up. Maria was the most important female figure during Picasso's childhood, but Picasso may not have been Picasso if not for his father's refusal to abide by longstanding custom.

Years earlier, Don José Ruiz y Blasco was a directionless young man trying to develop his artistic talents and make a living by painting. He was unable to earn a living from his art, however. He eventually went to live with one of his brothers, Pablo Ruiz y Blasco, a doctor of theology and canon of the Malaga Cathedral. Pablo's residence was located in one of Malaga's most important neighborhoods, the Plaza de la Merced, a large town square that surrounded an elaborate garden. Another family lived in the Plaza de la Merced at the same time—the Picasso family. For years, the Ruiz family and the Picassos knew one another.

In time, José's ten brothers and sisters decided it was time for him to take a wife and settle down. They wanted him to abandon his dreams of becoming a successful artist. Also, none

word for pencil. Maria claims he asked for one constantly. Once he had a pencil in hand, the toddler "covered entire sheets of paper with elaborate spirals, which, he managed to indicate to admiring relatives, were *torruellas*—spun sugar cakes."[11] In his adult art, Picasso used these spirals over and over again.

With his early interest in pencil and paper, Don José had high hopes his son might become an artist and follow in his footsteps. (José's father had been a middle-class merchant, an occupation that never appealed to José.) Pablo's father began giving him formal instruction in art and drawing when his son was only six or seven. Picasso took to these studies with a keen

of José's siblings had produced any children, and they hoped he could pass on the family name to children of his own. His brothers and sisters selected a young Picasso daughter to be José's bride. The family was acceptable to the Ruiz clan, and everyone believed the two were a good match—everyone except José.

He was not interested in the young girl his siblings picked for him. Instead, he fell in love with one of her cousins, whom he met through his chosen bride. Even then, though, José did not marry immediately. He waited another two years before taking Maria Picasso Lopez as his wife. The following year, their first child was born. He would be christened in a local church and named according to Spanish custom. Although his name would be lengthy and include the names of "various godparents, relatives, and saints,"* the child's first name—Pablo—would give honor to the Catholic priest who had provided a temporary home to Don José, the infant's father.

* Lael Wertenbaker, *The World of Picasso, 1881–1973* (Amsterdam: Time-Life Books, 1984), 8.

interest. He soon became obsessed with art, at the expense of the rest of his studies. According to the artist, he never learned his ABCs in the proper order. He also claimed that he graduated from grammar school only "because a kindly Malaga schoolmaster supplied him with the answers he required to pass an arithmetic test."[12]

Although many of the paintings and other artwork created by Picasso's father was second rate, almost amateurish, he proved himself to be a good teacher to his young son. As a Spanish painter, he had an intense love of realism but was willing to experiment. Don José once bought a plaster head of a Greek goddess on which he painted a realistic face, recreating the female head as a religious image after Our Lady of Sorrows. He even added hair for eyebrows and painted golden tears running down her cheeks. The adult Picasso remembered the art experiment as "always very ugly,"[13] but the point was to experiment with materials and mediums in new ways. It was a lesson Pablo Picasso never forgot.

Don José taught other lessons to his young prodigy; these would help mold him into the artist he would become:

> Other useful tricks were observed by the watchful eye of his son. In his passion for painting pigeons, Don Jose would often attempt ambitious compositions. In order to arrive at the happiest solution in their arrangement, he would first paint individual birds on paper, then having cut them out, he shifted them round until the composition took shape. In fact, from his childhood Pablo became acquainted with the possibilities of using material in unconventional ways, borrowing from any source that came to hand, and making the newly discovered substance obey his wishes. Brushes and paint were by no means the only tools of the trade; knives, scissors, pins and paste all played their part.[14]

Early drawings of Picasso's childhood survive today. These

sketches portray simple objects the budding artist saw around him, including pigeons, which were a favorite in his father's artwork. Don José kept models of pigeons for his own paintings, and Picasso sketched these over and over again. Young Pablo became so proficient at sketching his subject that he could "start from any point—the belly of a horse or the tail of a burro—and in one continuous line produce a remarkable likeness of the beast."[15] He could do the same by using scissors and cutting out his subject in exact likeness.

Another popular subject of Picasso's childhood art was the bullfight, an important Spanish pastime. Don José took him to bullfights when he was so young that Pablo could attend for free, since he could sit on his father's lap. The first time Picasso attempted an oil painting, his subject was of a crowd that was watching a picador at a bullfight. (A *picador* is a horseman who uses a lance to stab the bull's neck muscles so the animal keeps its head down when the matador enters the bullring.) Pablo was eight or nine when he painted the picador picture, and he kept this early painting for the rest of his life. (Picasso's sister, Lola, damaged the painting, though, when she was only five or six by jabbing a nail through the eyes.)

Bullfighting would remain one of Picasso's passions throughout his life—it served as a recurring subject in his art. At age 17, he created his first copperplate etching by portraying a picador in the bullring. In his first attempt, he forgot that the print from the etching would be a reverse image. This meant his picador would be shown with his lance in his left hand. Young Picasso shrugged off the error and named his etching, *El Zurdo (The Left-handed One)*. Remembering his early bullfighting art, Picasso admitted: "People think that I painted the pictures of bullfights in those days after they were over. Not at all. I painted them the day before and sold them to anyone so as to have enough money to buy a ticket."[16]

A FAMILY MOVE

Pablo Picasso's first ten years were happy, filled with love, and the possibilities were endless for the future artist. Change was coming to his family, however. Working as an art teacher, Don José never made much money, and these were difficult years financially for him and his family. He had three children—another daughter, Concepcion, was born in 1887, when Pablo was six. Concepcion would not survive into adulthood but died at age ten after struggling with diphtheria for three years. Prior to her death, Don José recognized that the family house was getting too crowded, and he was forced to make a serious decision. He decided to move his family and leave Malaga to take a position with the Instituto da Guarda, a secondary school of fine arts, in the town of La Coruña. The family's move from Malaga was a sad one. Both Maria and José's families had lived in the Spanish Mediterranean town for several generations. They were leaving family and friends behind. For Don José, the move "brought to an end the quiet life of well-established habits that he had enjoyed, and severed contacts on which he had come to depend for help and advice."[17] It was a sad September day in 1891 for both Maria and José when they boarded a ship with their three children bound for their new home.

Although La Coruña and Malaga were both Spanish port cities, they were very different. La Coruña was 700 miles northwest of Malaga, situated on the Atlantic, not the sunny Mediterranean. Malaga had been a place of wonderful warmth and almost constant sunlight. La Coruña was a city dominated by fog and rain for a good part of the year. Ten-year-old Pablo Picasso watched as his father's sadness over leaving Malaga continued after their move. Picasso remembered how Don José became depressed and nearly lifeless. His father would spend hours staring out windows watching the ceaseless patter of an Iberian rain. He painted less and less, and often left his works unfinished. Sometimes, young Pablo would finish his father's paintings for him. One story tells of Don José returning from

One of Picasso's most important works during his early teens is *Girl with Bare Feet*, which he completed in 1895. Currently on display at the Musée Picasso in Paris, the oil painting reflects Picasso's early desire to capture human form and personality.

a walk in the city to find his son had finished one of his pigeon sketches. By the story, Pablo's detail was so rich and delicate that "Don Jose handed his own palette and brushes to his son, then 13, and vowed never to paint again."[18] Art historians, though, are not certain the story is true.

One reality was true: Young Pablo Picasso was revealing more and more talent and a greater interest in art with each passing year. He filled notebooks and sketch pads with an endless variety of subjects. He walked every street of La Coruña, searching for interesting sites to sketch. He drew the harbor of La Coruña, as well as the endless beach, the cityscape, and the surrounding countryside, many times. Pablo also completed several portraits of his sister, Lola. One of his most famous paintings of his early teen years is titled *Girl with Bare Feet*, which he completed in 1895 at the age of 14. (The girl in the painting, however, is not Lola, but a young model.) The work already shows his mastery of the canvas and his skill with oils and brush. Although he was only a teenager, he painted and sketched with the confidence of an experienced adult. He worked very fast, very deliberately, and almost never changed anything once he committed it to canvas or paper. At about the same age, he produced a portrait of his mother in profile using pastels and crayons. It is a loving, thoughtful portrait, which presents a seated Maria as a plump patrician, fashionable, well groomed, and dozing.

Picasso's family lived in La Coruña for nearly four years. Then, in 1895, his father was offered a teaching position at the School of Fine Arts in Barcelona. Don José did not hesitate to accept the opportunity to leave La Coruña. Before the move, the family paid a visit to family and friends back in Malaga. Picasso's aunts and uncles made a great fuss over him, this young, talented boy of 14. They had come to believe in him and regarded him as an artistic genius. One of his uncles paid models to pose while Pablo sketched and painted. An aunt, outfitted in a fur coat, posed on a hot summer's day. The support Pablo Picasso received was endless.

Soon, Barcelona was home to the family of Don José and Maria. The family had returned once more to life in the Mediterranean. Barcelona was a thriving city, an ancient city-state established by Phoenician traders thousands of years earlier. The city served as the heart and soul of the region of

Catalonia. For hundreds of years, since the Middle Ages, the Catalans had "enjoyed political independence, economic prosperity, and a flourishing art."[19] In the midst of the 1890s, many Catalans were interested in a new intellectual movement, *modernismo*—a social theory that rejected the materialism brought on by the ever advancing progress of the Industrial Revolution. The movement was as important among local artists and writers as to any other group in the region. In time, it became a branch of the Art Nouveau movement, which became popular by the turn of the twentieth century, both in Europe and the United States. Several of its founders, including Ramón Casas, were Catalan artists. He would eventually show an interest in the artistic works of young Pablo Picasso. Don José, however, was not part of the movement. He knew little about this philosophical and artistic redirection. Even after the move, he was not much happier in Barcelona than he had been in La Coruña.

The teenaged Picasso could not have been happier, however. Barcelona was alive with movement, ideas, politics, and art. He came to love the city and its people. As an adult, Picasso identified with the city so intensely that many Spaniards believed the famous artist was born there. In later years, whenever the great painter became "homesick," it was for Barcelona.

No sooner did the family settle down in their new city that Pablo began to study at the School of Fine Arts, where Don José taught. In fact, his father managed to get Pablo enrolled in advanced classes, even though he was younger than his classmates. Young Picasso did have to submit a pair of charcoal drawings of a live model to a panel of art teachers before he was allowed entry into the advanced art program. He completed the sketches within a week. Students usually worked a month on these two important sketches. (The drawings are still part of the school's archival collection.) The sketches were good enough to earn Pablo a seat in the advanced class. To encourage his son's art education, Don José rented a small room near the family home for Pablo to work on his own, away from distractions. Despite his intentions, Don José stopped by Pablo's rented room five or six times a day and even graded his son's sketches. Young Pablo came to resent his father's criticisms, and arguments between the two became common.

It was undeniable that Pablo Picasso's artistic talent was advancing. At age 15, he exhibited a painting at the National Exhibition of Fine Arts in Madrid. The work—titled *Science and Charity*—took an honorable mention. (Pablo included his father in the work, posing him as a medical doctor.) Later, when the painting was entered in a competition in Malaga, it took a gold medal. Young Picasso's future seemed clearly to lie

BEING HISPANIC

THE ROOT OF PICASSO'S ARTISTIC SPIRIT

The annals of Western art history are filled with the contributions of hundreds, perhaps even thousands of artists, including painters and sculptors. Among those considered to have made some of the most significant contributions are several of Spanish descent, including Picasso.

For hundreds of years, Spanish artists, from Velázquez to Ribera to Goya, played their role on the artistic stage, each bringing their unique talents and view of the world to their art. Picasso is counted as one of the most significant among them. Despite spending the vast majority of his adult life in France, Picasso always remained, in his work and in his approach to life, a Spaniard. He was always keenly aware of his ethnicity, of how a Spaniard lives life to the fullest, with an energy rooted in a love of life itself.

Even when he was cut off from his homeland, Picasso never lost his love of Spain. His friends always recalled that, when Picasso spoke nostalgically of home, he always meant Spain, especially Barcelona. When the Fascists drove the Republican government from power, and Francisco Franco installed himself as dictator, Picasso made the personal

within the art world. His father decided his son should receive a better art education and sent him to the most renowned art school in Spain—the Royal Academy of San Fernando, in Madrid. One of his father's brothers agreed to provide the boy with financial support, and, in 1897, Picasso left home, at age 16, for the Spanish capital.

Shortly after Picasso arrived at the Royal Academy, he stopped attending class. He was already forming his own artistic mind, and the formal schooling did not interest him. He did not, however, abandon his art. Madrid was an exciting city, where various types of art flourished. It was the largest city in which young Picasso had ever lived, and he spent much of his

commitment never to return to his native land as long Franco ruled. It was one of the hardest decisions Picasso ever made. To take such a stand, he knew he would be cut off from the land of his birth, the land that had helped form his identity as a creative Hispanic artist.

Today, Barcelona remains the embodiment of Picasso's artistic spirit. Here in this great ancient Iberian city stands one of the greatest repositories of art by the country's native son—the Picasso Museum. Originally housed in a fifteenth-century Gothic palace, near where he lived as a hungry, young artist, the museum's collection includes hundreds of his works, largely through contributions made by Jaime Sabartés, who donated more than 400 pieces of art, as well as gifts made by Picasso himself. The museum was part of the gifted Spanish painter's effort to make Spain the natural home for his paintings, sculptures, and other art.

Ironically, it may have been his love of Spain that drove Picasso to spend much of his adult life in southern France. Given his self-imposed exile through the Franco years, he could, along the French Riviera, experience—despite being slightly removed geographically—the warm waters of the Mediterranean; the soft, diffused light of the south; the gently undulating lifestyle found otherwise in so many of the ancient cities of Iberia; and the slow, yet passion-driven rhythms of his birth, his people, his home—his Spain.

time wandering its streets, shops, cafés, and neighborhoods, even those that were among the city's poorest. He found inspiration for his artwork at every turn and on every street corner. He also made frequent visits to the Prado, one of Madrid's most important art museums, a complex containing some of Spain's greatest art treasures; works created by Spain's most talented masters, including the Romantic painters Velázquez, Zurbaran, and Goya. Among his favorite Spanish painters was the seventeenth-century master El Greco. The Baroque artist had created a unique style of painting that included bright colors, exaggerated physical forms, and a religious mysticism, all of which Picasso appreciated. He copied El Greco's style and sent sketches for his father to see. Don José was not pleased. El Greco's works had fallen out of favor with the formal, nineteenth-century art world of Spain. "You are following the bad way,"[20] the father wrote back to his son.

Soon, young Picasso was living a difficult life in Madrid. His uncle cut off his support when he learned Pablo had dropped out of the Royal Academy, and his father could not afford to send him much money. Picasso lived poorly, unable to afford paint and canvas. He could barely afford drawing paper. He drew as much as he could, though, filling the pages of his sketch pads with images of the people he met: simple street folk, vagabonds, and those he shared drink with in local cafés and bars.

Within a year of his arrival in Madrid, Picasso became ill with scarlet fever, which caused him to abandon life in the city and move to a small Catalonian village, Horta de San Juan. For the first time in his life, Pablo Picasso was living in a rural setting. There he came in contact with a new group of downtrodden people—peasants and farmers—whose faces became his new subjects. He worked alongside them, milking cows and handling oxen and mules. Picasso "began to understand the human struggle against the forces of nature."[21] After a year of recovery, Picasso returned to city life but not in Madrid. Instead, he returned to Barcelona. Before him stood his future.

He was a 17-year-old man, ready to meet the challenges of the world through his art:

> His essential character was forged, the pattern of his life plain-
> ly set. He could be ruthless or gentle, gregarious or withdrawn.
> He combined prankish gaiety with a sense of human tragedy,
> moods of elation with moods of black despair. Acutely sensi-
> tive, he was open to all manner of ideas—but on his own
> terms, for he was too ruggedly independent to submit to the
> dominance of others.[22]

He scraped together enough money to buy inexpensive sketch books and filled their pages with the faces of the lower class: common people, including dock workers, cabaret singers, dancehall girls, other artists, and prostitutes. When he could afford it, he went to the bullfights and sketched more scenes of the ring. He continued to be influenced by the works of El Greco. Picasso lived with other struggling artists, sharing studios and living almost as poorly as he did in Madrid. He made friends with other free spirits and creative talents of the Spanish avant-garde. One of their common gathering places was a café known as *Els Quatre Gats*, which translates from Catalan to "The Four Cats." At the tables of the tavern, artists, including Picasso, discussed their work and their theories of art, especially modernismo. On the walls of "The Four Cats," Picasso and these unknown artists hung their paintings, wait-ing to be noticed, waiting to become known.

Now that he was back in Barcelona, Picasso could see his family once more. He visited them almost every day. The works of art he showed his family were simple, middle-class pictures of conventional subjects. He did not share his more startling subject matter. Although he seemed to continue to solicit his father's approval, his father no longer had any significant impact on his art.

In February 1900, the owner of Els Quatre Gats featured a special exhibition of Picasso's artwork. The exhibit earned him some critical attention. One critic, writing about the Picasso show, described young Pablo as "hardly more than a child," but described him as having an "extraordinary facility in the use of brush and pencil."[23] Even as Picasso was beginning to gain some attention for his art and talent, though, he was becoming restless and began considering moving to another city, perhaps in England. That fall, he made a trip to London with a classmate from the School of Fine Arts. While traveling, he and his companion passed through Paris, which was then considered one of the most important art centers in Western Europe. The City of Light was a mecca for young, energetic, and experimental artists. Once there, Picasso fell in love with the city. Paris, in time, would become his new home, changing his art and his artistic future forever.

3

The Blue Period

France was the first foreign country Picasso visited and he arrived in Paris just a few days short of his nineteenth birthday. He discovered the ancient French capital in the midst of a transitional period in the worlds of literature and art. The city had become a haven for innovative painters, intellectuals, and writers. The key to their new artistic and literary styles was radicalism. This movement, centered in the City of Light at the Fin de Siècle (end of the century), found its inspiration in the decadent underworld of Parisian life. The taverns, cafés, brothels, artist studios, and politically driven communes throughout the city served as places where artists and writers could share ideas and express their new views.

It was a world inhabited by political radicals, prostitutes, alcoholics, and drug addicts. Its inhabitants constantly pushed the limits of acceptable social custom and public activity. Among many, sewer rats became trendy pets. Onstage, it was common for women to perform bare breasted. Prostitution was romanticized in the literature. Although homosexuality and lesbianism were culturally and morally taboo, they were a common and accepted part of the bohemian lifestyle of these artists and writers. Depression, personal demons, and suicide were not uncommon. Not only were these activities acceptable, but some even considered such sufferings a necessary part of the artistic lifestyle of the period. Decadence became the standard for this avant-garde movement, which hoped to redefine the parameters of fashionable art and accepted social practice. The "Fin de Siècle Paris" movement, culturally speaking, lasted only until around 1905; by that time, it had burned out by excess. The impact of the movement, however, was its continuing influence on art and literature throughout much of the rest of the twentieth century. As for Picasso, he was not only drawn to that world, but he provided part of its artistic momentum.

On his first visit to Paris, Picasso immediately found friends and a place to work. He was aware of a colony of artists, several of them Spaniards, who lived in the Montmartre quarter of Paris, located on the northern edge of the city. It was a romantically run-down neighborhood, "spread on terraced hillsides where windmills had turned and grapevines ripened not long before. Narrow cobbled streets and muddy alleys climbed precipitously between warrens of tenements that were freezing in winter and stifling in summer."[24] To escape the harshness of poverty, many residents of Montmartre frequented the local taverns, cafés, and dance halls "where a few francs bought food, warmth and entertainment."[25] Here the young artist took residence, and fellow painters introduced him to these cafés and taverns, and to the important museums, galleries, and art dealers. For 19-year-old Picasso, he was, for the moment, in the middle of an artistic movement that swept him along, and he was intent on enjoying the ride. He had arrived in Paris just in time.

There was no place in the world like Paris at the turn of the twentieth century. It was the home of one of the greatest museums in all of Europe, the Louvre, which Picasso would visit often. There was the Trocadero Museum, where Picasso was introduced to African art, which would have a lifelong influence on his own art. He frequented such social outlets as the Cabaret des Quat'z Arts and the famous dancehall, the Moulin de la Galette. For Picasso, there was no other place he wanted to be:

> The life of Paris by day and by night, the streets glittering under the warm autumn rain, the din from market stalls and the clatter of horse-drawn traffic on the stones, enchanted Picasso and made him feel at home. . . . Here he recognized an atmosphere which would foster his development. He had come from Barcelona to escape the cramping influence of his family and the burden of provincial life. He was in search of a society which would in the widest sense nourish his ambitions as a painter, and he wished to see for himself the achievements of the past and promise for the future that this much talked of Mecca of the arts had to offer.[26]

There was work for Picasso in Montmartre. A local Catalan painter provided him with a studio along the narrow Rue Gabrielle, and Picasso found a patron, a Barcelonan named Père Manyac, who agreed to pay him 150 francs (about $30) a month for any of his artwork. Though it was not much, it provided the young artist with money for his art supplies and allowed him to lead a meager lifestyle. All that mattered to him was that he was working in Paris. Over time, Picasso became so popular with his fellow artists in the Barcelona colony of Montmartre that the group became known as *la bande a Picasso*—"Picasso's Crew."

Although Paris remained a constant adventure for Picasso as he explored the city through the fall of 1900, he went home to celebrate Christmas with his family, as he had promised his father he would. The short reunion was not pleasant. Don José was somewhat displeased with his son's appearance—his disheveled clothing, his long hair—but he was very disappointed in Pablo's new paintings. The old-fashioned father-artist had no appreciation for the world of the impressionists and the emerging expressionists, both of whom were having an impact on his son's work. Other visits to family members in Malaga (where he spent New Year's) and Barcelona also did not go well. In addition, Picasso's artist traveling companion, fellow Spaniard Carles Casagemas, was struggling with depression and drinking heavily (his girlfriend had left him), and appeared to be on the verge of suicide. Away from Paris, distracted by family problems and the struggles of Casagemas, Picasso lost his employment with Manyac. By spring, Picasso was ready to escape family and his suicidal friend and return to Paris. His relationship with his family, especially with his father, had continued to deteriorate. As a result, he stopped using "Ruiz" when he signed his signature and chose, for the rest of his life, to sign his name, simply "Picasso." It was his mother's name.

With Picasso back in Paris, Manyac began to support him again and even introduced Picasso to another art dealer, Ambroise Vollard. "A tall man with a high, domed forehead, full cheeks and a tiny, pursed mouth,"[27] Vollard liked Picasso's work. Through his extensive connections with wealthy art collectors and museum curators, Vollard became important to the advancement of Picasso's career. In earlier years, he had helped Cézanne, one of the great impressionists, develop his career. He had had an influence on Degas, Renoir, Gauguin, and the sculptor Rodin. He immediately offered the young Spanish painter a public show along with a Basque painter named Iturrino. Still only nineteen, Picasso was introduced to art critics and an art-purchasing audience. This first exhibition of Picasso's artwork in Paris at the gallery of Ambroise Vollard opened in June 1901 and was well received. A critic writing for one of the popular avant-garde magazines was glowing in his review:

Picasso is a painter, absolutely and beautifully . . . Like all pure painters he adores colour in itself and to him each substance has its own colour. Also he is in love with every subject and to him everything is a subject; the flowers that gush forth furiously from a vase towards the light, the vase alone, and the table that carries the vase and the luminous air that dances around.[28]

The Vollard exhibition brought Picasso into a lifelong friendship with poet Max Jacob, the son of a Jewish tailor, who took an immediate liking to Picasso and his art. At first their relationship was difficult, because Picasso spoke Spanish and Jacob was French. In time, though, after meeting almost daily, Picasso learned to speak French and became quite fluent. When Picasso later fell on hard times, he shared an apartment with Jacob.

Despite the supportive reviews Picasso received from the Vollard exhibition, by the fall of 1901, he was beginning to change his style. His earlier works often featured bright colors. He switched to more sober, even somber shades in his painting. In his earlier works, he often mimicked the styles of other painters, especially important impressionists and post-impressionists, such as Degas, Van Gogh, and Gauguin. But, at age 20, he was slipping into a mature individuality in his painting. He began to paint in an expressive style all his own.

DARKNESS ENTERS PICASSO'S LIFE AND WORK

This new stylistic approach would influence Picasso's paintings for the next three years. Art historians generally refer to these years as Picasso's "Blue Period." For much of this period of time, Picasso gave up his life in Paris. Driven by a lack of money and the fact that he was sometimes so poor he was nearly starving, he left for Spain with the approach of winter in 1901. He did make a short visit to Paris during the fall of 1902, but otherwise, he remained in Spain until 1904.

Between 1901 and 1904, many of his paintings were

dominated by various shades of blue. As for subjects, he was a poverty-stricken artist who painted poverty-stricken people. Typically, his subjects were drug addicts, alcoholics, prostitutes, and aged men and women who lived desperate lives and shuddered through existences lined with poverty and despair. Perhaps Picasso, himself, was blue. His friend Casagemas had, at 9 P.M. on February 17, 1901, finally given into his alcoholic-driven depression and shot himself in a Paris wine shop by placing a pistol to his right temple. The death by suicide of his close friend shocked Picasso and set him on a course of his own depression.

His paintings were not selling well, and he had abandoned his old style. Although the light, airy, and colorful works of the impressionists had inspired him the previous year, his paintings now took on a dark element, "an all-pervading blue."[29]

Art historians have struggled with the question of why Picasso rejected the brightness and lightness of the impressionists and persisted in painting in blue shades. Some have suggested that because he was so poor, he could not afford a wide array of colors. That theory hardly seems likely. Others have speculated that he was rejecting the natural yellows, browns, and ochers found in the landscapes of Spain, and that blue was a welcome change in color. Again, there seems to be no basis for this theory. Most likely, he was motivated by his personal mood and personal thematic agendas during those still formative years. Before he left for Barcelona late in 1901, his friends "noticed a change in his humour, he became morose."[30] He was attempting to portray desperation, sorrow, hopelessness, and anonymous pain. Through these paintings, Picasso revealed his "compassion for the destitute, the blind and the lame, the outcasts of Paris society whose harsh lot he shared."[31]

Among these paintings are those considered important in the development of Picasso's art, despite his struggle with depression and poverty. They include a portrait of a drug addict, *The Absinthe Drinker* (1901), which portrays a lonely

One of Picasso's most famous pieces from his Blue Period is *The Absinthe Drinker*. The subject of this 1901 painting reflects Picasso's dark mood at the time: a lonely, blue-cloaked woman is sitting by herself at a café table, flanked by a bottle of absinthe (a strong herbal liqueur popular in Paris at the time).

woman at a café table, shrouded in a deep blue cloak, as if in death, and flanked by a table and a single glass of her drug of choice. Another work, *Evocation* (1901), depicts, in allegorical fashion, the burial of his friend Casagemas, with its blue-clad mourners bent over the corpse, which is clothed in a white winding sheet. There is also a view of heaven that includes the soul of Casagemas riding through a rolling blue sky on a white horse, surrounded by female nudes, some of whom wear blue stockings. There are various portraits of somber, tired, and lonesome subjects—Carlota Valdivia (later renamed *Celestina*; 1904), his friend Jaime Sabartés (1901, 1904), as well as himself, in *Self-Portrait with Overcoat* (1901). Perhaps most famous today are two works of his Blue Period, *La Vie* (Life), and *The Old Guitarist*, both painted in 1903. In *The Old Guitarist*, Picasso is beginning to alter his presentation of the human body, choosing to distort his figure to portray his subject's sad physical decay. There is an element of El Greco in the work, shown in the aged guitarist's elongated fingers and limbs. Blue dominates the work, shading everything from foreground to background, except for the body of the guitar, which is painted realistically in a muted earth tone. Not even Picasso could have known at the time, but this painting probably serves as the forerunner to later still-life works he would create in the cubist style.

As for *La Vie*, it serves as a mystically driven allegory and message about the universal struggle of existence. The painting is large, standing more than six feet tall and more than four feet wide. Two pairs of figures—a nearly naked young man and woman on the left and a mother and infant child on the right—face one another, both giving the appearance of suffering and hopelessness. In the hands of a depressed Picasso, even in these symbols of human joy and hope—physical love between a man and woman and the love of a mother toward her child—there is no joy. Between the two pairs of subjects is a pair of portraits, both of nudes, each mirroring the sorrow and despair of the couple and the mother. Picasso's message does not appear to be subtle. The painting is about life, but also it "is apparently about love—mother love, sexual love, platonic love, self-love and perhaps even more specifically about the unhappiness of love."[32] Yet, as sorrow dominates the canvas, there is an innocent contentment on the face of the mother's sleeping child, who is securely held in her arms, warmly wrapped in a blanket.

Whether Picasso intended to include this small symbol of future hope or not, *La Vie* provided some personal hope for the despondent artist. Of all his Blue Period paintings, it became one of the most important. Unlike most of his other blue-based works, *La Vie* became an artistic sensation and financial success for Picasso. He painted the work in Barcelona in May 1903, and it sold by the following month, within just a few days of its completion. The buyer was a Parisian art dealer and collector, Jean Saint-Gaudens. The purchase of *La Vie* did not go unnoticed by the Barcelona public. The sale of the large painting is mentioned in an article in a Barcelona newspaper, *Liberal*, dated June 4, 1903.

There were few buyers for Picasso's other paintings, though, and he missed the life he had found the previous year in Paris. By the spring of 1904, he decided to return to Paris with no intentions of ever leaving this artistic center. With no more money than when he left the city two-and-a-half years earlier, he bought a third-class train ticket and headed north. Back in the Montmartre district, he took residence in a run-down house at 13 Rue Ravignan. He would live there for five years and, despite his poverty, would always remember those years as his happiest. He sold paintings sporadically, mostly to Vollard, but he continued to live a meager existence.

Despite his poverty, Picasso loved his return to Paris life. He reconnected with old friends and made new ones. Among them was a young woman named Fernande Olivier. She and Picasso would become lovers and remain such until 1912. She would pose for him many times, serving as a model.

THE ROSE PERIOD

Once Picasso settled into a routine after returning to Paris, he found great contentment in his life. He was happier, he had a female companion, and he was selling paintings from time to time. His mood changed, bringing an end to his Blue Period, only to replace it with another, one recognized by art historians as his Rose Period. Not only did his works take on a new, lighter hue based on various reddish and pinkish shades, but his subject matter generally changed as well. Whereas his Blue Period had been dominated by such subjects as prostitutes, lonely men, and despair, in his Rose Period, which lasted from 1905 to 1906, his new subjects were lighter, mostly circus performers. His painted world of sorrow and depression gave way to a happier, dreamier state that was filled with acrobats, jugglers, clowns, and other circus people. Much of the isolation depicted by his bluish paintings of one lonely person per canvas was replaced by groups of people.

PICASSO AND FERNANDE

The first thing that drew young, exciting Fernande Olivier to Picasso was the artist's piercing black eyes. Before they became lovers, Fernande lived within the bohemian circle of artists and writers who lived in and around 13 Rue Ravignan in Paris. The address was a dilapidated tenement house, which Max Jacob dubbed le bateau-lavoir—a name for the local laundry barges that Jacob thought the apartment building resembled. Fernande was the daughter of a manufacturer of artificial flowers. Earlier, she had married a sculptor, who, unfortunately, went insane.

Fernande first noticed Picasso on a sultry summer's day in 1904 as she stood in line at the outdoor water pump she and her fellow residents shared. She felt him staring at her with those dark, piercing eyes. Despite his eyes, Fernande did not find Picasso particularly attractive. She, on the other hand, was a handsome woman, "young and striking, with auburn hair and green eyes."* On another summer's day, as she ran into the bateau-lavoir to escape a sudden rainstorm, Picasso stood in the entrance, holding a kitten. The two met, and the artist invited

For inspiration, Picasso attended the Medrano Circus with his artistic and literary friends. Among Picasso's most famous Rose Period circus works is his watercolor and crayon composition *The Acrobat Family* (1905), which presents a touching family scene of a circus couple and their infant, with a monkey, that "introduces an element of surprise and gives the painting symbolic weight."[33] Another is a portrait of a group of circus performers, the *Family of Saltimbanques* (1905). (*Saltimbanques* is a French word meaning "buffoon.") The giant painting stretches seven feet high and seven feet wide. It includes five circus people, including a harlequin whose profile is that of Picasso himself. Although the painting does not center on a focused familial relationship, the work is bold and

her into his apartment to show her a pet mouse he kept in a bureau drawer, as well as his stack of blue-hued paintings. This off-chance meeting developed into a relationship, and Fernande soon moved in with Picasso.

Their relationship was less than equal, however. Picasso could be extremely chauvinistic and expected his lover to constantly cook for him and his friends. He gave her a meager two francs a day to make their meals, which was barely enough to cover the expenses. While Picasso would sit with male friends and talk endlessly, Fernande was expected to remain out of the conversation. When he painted, Picasso also expected her to remain quiet. The Spanish painter exerted a great amount of control over her. In fact, he would not even allow her to leave their flat without him and would lock her in to keep her at home.

* Lael Wertenbaker, *The World of Picasso, 1881–1973* (Amsterdam: Time-Life Books, 1984), 35.

Picasso

One of Picasso's most notable Rose Period pieces is *The Acrobat Family*. Painted in 1905, this watercolor and crayon composition depicts a circus family and their infant, along with a monkey. During the Rose Period, Picasso moved away from the somberness of the Blue Period and focused instead on delicate and lighter subjects and colors.

enigmatic. Picasso began work on the oil painting in 1904 and finished it in 1905. During the months he worked on the painting, he changed the composition of the people several times. (X rays of the work reveal that he originally placed many more people in the painting, then reduced the number to two, only to increase it again to a half dozen.) Other important Rose Period works are his *Boy Leading a Horse* (1905–1906) and several portraits of Fernande, mostly nudes.

By 1905, in the midst of his Rose Period, Picasso's inventory of Blue Period paintings was beginning to find buyers. One of the most important was an American living in France, Gertrude Stein, a radical and experimental writer, who befriended many of the great artists and writers in Paris during the early twentieth century, including Paul Cézanne, Henri Matisse, Pierre-Auguste Renoir, and Ernest Hemingway. She and her four siblings had inherited a fortune from their father, who had made his money in the clothing business, railroads, mines, and the stock market. She and two of her brothers, Leo and Michael, collected an amazing inventory of paintings by budding artists before they became famous. Leo bought his first Picasso in 1905, a Blue Period work depicting an adolescent nude girl carrying a basket of flowers. *Young Girl with a Basket of Flowers* would be the first of an entire collection of Picasso's works the Steins would acquire. Soon after this purchase (which was made through an art dealer), the Steins visited Picasso's studio and bought several of his paintings, spending an incredible 800 francs, "more money than Picasso had ever seen at one time in his life."[34]

The Steins were crucial to Picasso's future. Their purchases of his work pulled him out of his poverty (he would never be truly poor again), and they introduced him to other art collectors, who began buying his work. These included a wealthy Russian named Sergei Shchukin and a German art lover, Wilhelm Uhde.

As for Gertrude Stein, Picasso, after meeting her, was struck by her almost mannish appearance and wanted to paint her. Picasso did not ask her himself, though. Instead, he commissioned one of his art dealers, Clovis Sagot, who was a former circus clown, to "ask her if she will pose for me."[35] She agreed, and the result was one of the most famous portraits painted by Picasso. The story behind the portrait is magical:

> Soon Picasso and the Steins were exchanging frequent visits—at the Steins' flat on the Rue de Fleurus for Saturday soirees and at Picasso's studio on weekday afternoons for Gertrude's sittings for her portrait. Day after day she traveled across the city to Montmartre, going part way on a horse-drawn bus and climbing the steep hills to the *bateau lavoir* on foot. While Gertrude posed and Picasso painted, Fernande, who had a beautiful voice, read aloud the fables of La Fontaine. The usually voluble Gertrude used the time to her own advantage. Later she revealed she had "meditated and made sentences" for a story she was writing.[36]

But after Gertrude had sat through 80 or 90 sittings, Picasso suddenly erased her face from his canvas. He claimed he could no longer "see" Gertrude. For the moment, he abandoned the portrait, and left Paris to vacation with Fernande in the Pyrenees, which border southern France and northern Spain. When he returned to Paris that fall, he took up painting the portrait of Gertrude once again. This time, he painted a new head, ultimately creating a portrait in two styles. Everything he had painted, except for the face, had been done with a level of realism. The face, though, was another matter. It was flat, reminiscent of a primitive African mask. Her eyes were shaped like almonds. The look was totally different, totally new. When the work was completed, Stein's friends claimed the face did not resemble hers at all. "Never mind," said Picasso, all-knowingly. "She will come to look like that."[37] The portrait would mark the beginning of Picasso's style of recasting the human body and its features into unique images born of his inspired creation.

Cubism

The year was 1906, a turning point in the early career of the artist Pablo Picasso. The 24-year-old painter's work was beginning to become popular. Admirers and collectors were buying his paintings, thanks in part to his agent, Ambroise Vollard. (Picasso also owed a great deal to the Steins, as well.) He was not only selling his work, but the price of an individual painting was also increasing. At last, his artistic endeavors were paying off, and a lack of money would never plague Picasso again. (As for Fernande, he was able to keep her in fancy hats, furs, and expensive perfumes—three of her personal passions.) The future seemed to belong to Picasso.

That same year, in March, Picasso's world was also changed by a meeting arranged through the Steins. On a Saturday evening, at Gertrude's flat, he met Henri Matisse, then the most well-known painter in Paris. The bearded, self-confident Matisse was 12 years older than Picasso, and his reputation as an artist was firmly established. When the younger Picasso met him, Matisse "looked every inch the master."[38] Unlike Picasso, Matisse had already established his career, first as an impressionist, and, by the early twentieth century, as a painter whose colors were extremely bold and whose subjects lay on the edge of realism. Matisse was leading the way in the transition of art from impressionism to a more expressive art known as fauvism. French fauvism flourished between 1898 and 1908, and relied heavily on pure, brilliant colors, sometimes daubed aggressively on the canvas, straight out of the paint tube. The result was an art style that moved beyond impressionism. Fauvists, like impressionists, still painted frequently from nature but filled their canvases with new, highly charged emotions. The year Matisse and Picasso met, fauvism was still experimental and shocking. The term *fauvism* was coined after one art critic referred to Matisse and his fellow expressionists as "Les Fauves," or "the Wild Beasts." The expressive work of Matisse had a direct impact on Picasso, and vice versa. Although their first encounter was cordial, the two men emerged from their meeting understanding that they were in competition to redirect the art world. Their friendship continued for years, but Matisse always kept track of Picasso's career, asking mutual friends about the Spaniard's latest works: "What is Pablo doing?"[39]

With money no longer a problem, Picasso gained a new economic freedom. He and Fernande went to Spain, visited family, and took time off from working in Paris, taking residence in the small village of Gósol, in the Pyrenees. He only stayed away from Paris for a matter of months, returning to the City of Light that August, after an outbreak of typhoid struck Gósol. During these months away from Paris, Picasso did not stop creating. Despite his newfound financial success as a painter in 1906, the year proved pivotal for his art in other ways, as well. Even as he was making a name for himself, he began to redefine his art, finding new inspirations. In Gósol, he began experimenting with primitivism. He was not alone. Other early-twentieth-century artists, including Matisse and Gauguin, were studying the primitive art of distant, non-

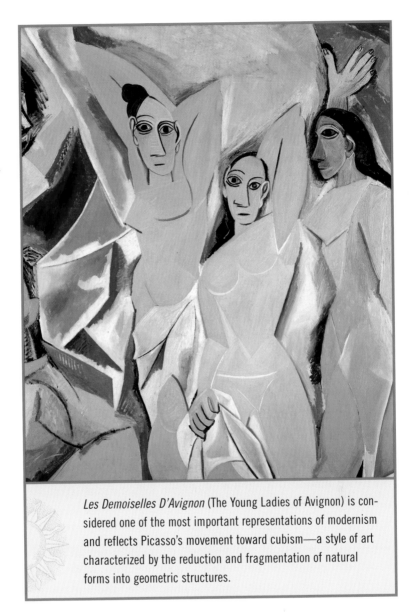

Les Demoiselles D'Avignon (The Young Ladies of Avignon) is considered one of the most important representations of modernism and reflects Picasso's movement toward cubism—a style of art characterized by the reduction and fragmentation of natural forms into geometric structures.

European cultures, especially those of Africa. Artwork from Africa, Asia, and the islands of the Pacific—mostly hand-carved statues—embodied, to artists like Picasso, a raw spirit, a primary source of artistic simplicity that was only rooted in realism but was not dependent on it. Painters like Matisse and Picasso were excited by primitivism's expressive energy and "sought to convey such qualities in their own figurative art."[40]

(Perhaps it had been this lure of primitivism that motivated Picasso to paint Gertrude Stein's head less realistically than he might have, otherwise.)

While in Gósol and inspired by primitivism, Picasso worked up 31 preliminary sketches done variously in most of the mediums in which he worked at the time: charcoal, pencil, pastel, watercolor, and oil. He was preparing a new painting, one that would reinvent his own art and the art of the Western world. He continued to work on this project into 1907, changing his subject matter and even changing his entire style. Primitivism continued to inspire him. He began planning his monumental work in the fall of 1906 and continued to make changes to the planned composition through May 1907. Picasso created 800 preliminary drawings and sketches before he began painting his final version of his groundbreaking painting *Les Demoiselles D'Avignon*, "The Young Ladies of Avignon."

His large, bold composition—it measures approximately seven feet in height and width—is a work featuring five nude women. Even though nudity in modern art was already well-established by the early twentieth century, Picasso presented his female nudes in a unique way. Three of the figures have faces and forms modified from a true reality, but he abandoned the true human face completely on the other two women by giving them faces and heads reminiscent of masks fashioned after African primitivism. In this work, Picasso brought together all the influences that were then swirling around him. In doing so, he created a unique artistic space. He distorted the human figures by painting them as a series of angles and flat shapes, turning them into subjects more nonhuman than human: Heads are turned 180 degrees, limbs are held at impossible angles, a leg and foot give way to a misshapen cube. The world these women inhabit is more surreal than real:

> [The painting] violated almost every precept of Western painting . . . Above all it did violence to the human form. Picasso

simply smashed the body to bits—making the canvas remind one critic of a "field of broken glass"—then put the pieces together again in a startling assemblage of angular planes, rounded wedges, facets of every shape. Not content with this heresy, he further defied anatomical principle by discarding ears, placing eyes at different levels; . . . he distorted one figure . . . so that her face and back both show . . . Were this all, the viewer's task would be perplexing enough. But at the same time Picasso is asking him to abandon his preconceived ideas of form, to forget natural appearances altogether, to look at the fragments that make up his nudes as pure forms in themselves.[41]

In recasting these five nude women on a completely different and unreal artistic landscape, Picasso was helping to create a new form of art: cubism—which would become one of the most important and revolutionary art movements of the twentieth century. It was so unique in its purpose that it completely distanced itself from every form of art that preceded it. As a modern art style, cubism created a unique approach to representing reality. Nearly all linear perspective was abandoned in favor of portraying an object, not from one artist's or viewer's perspective but from multiple views simultaneously. To complicate things, this technique was carried out on a two-dimensional surface. The result of looking at all sides at once and consolidating those into a combined, single view is a distorted, unrealistic image that sometimes reduced the subject to a combination of geometric patterns, such as cubes. *Les Demoiselles d'Avignon* serves as one of the first attempts by a modern artist to create a cubist canvas. Cubism would drive much of Picasso's art for the next seven years. He would return to the style many times over his lengthy art career.

This painting redefined art so dramatically that Picasso knew he could not present it in 1907 to the art-consuming public. He kept the innovative work in his studio for almost a decade, where it was seen only by a few people of Picasso's

During the summer of 1909, Picasso spent time in the remote Spanish mountain village of Horta de San Juan, where he painted several cubist works, including *Houses on a Hill*. In the painting, the houses of the village appear to be on top of one another and the sky blends with the houses in muted shades of browns and tans, which are accented with light blues, grays, and greens.

choosing. Even among close associates of Picasso, the painting was not acceptable. His friend Georges Braque, who was also a pioneer cubist, was one of the first to see the painting. He immediately criticized it, stating: "It is as though we are supposed to exchange our usual diet for one of tow and paraffin."[42] Another fauvist and friend of Picasso, André Derain, after seeing his painting, found it so disturbing that he told a friend that "one day we shall find Pablo has hanged himself behind his great canvas."[43] Matisse, when he viewed *Les Demoiselles d'Avignon*, despised it. For Matisse, his purpose in creating "fauvist" paintings was to appeal to his viewers and their sense of emotional pleasure. "It ridicules the modern movement," he concluded. "Which means primarily me!"[44] Picasso kept his avant-garde painting under wraps until he exhibited it publicly in 1916.

Despite a negative response from some of his closest artist friends, Picasso had created something new, bold, and innovative. He continued to apply cubism to his art. He spent his summer vacation in 1908 in the French village of Oise, 30 miles north of Paris. Here he dabbled with a type of cubism, working in the style of another innovative painter, Paul Cézanne. Cézanne's landscapes were experiments in recreating physical space by tinkering with true perspective, stripping the natural and manmade subjects of his paintings down to their barest elements. Likewise, during the summer of 1909, Picasso and Fernande made another trip to Spain and stayed in Horta de San Juan, where he and a friend had recovered from scarlet fever ten years earlier. While there, he produced another cubist painting, *Houses on a Hill* (1909). Through the painting, Picasso recreated the little village and its sparse panorama of simple, squarish buildings and homes into a series of stylized blocks, creating a cubist perspective in various muted shades of browns and tans, accented with light blues, grays, and greens. Art historians would later identify the landscape painting as an early stage of cubism known as analytical cubism.

In that year—1909—Picasso began to work closely with another innovative painter, the aforementioned Georges Braque, from Normandy. The two artists produced cubist works and shared criticisms of one another's compositions and style. Their styles became so similar that it was sometimes difficult to tell which artist had painted which canvas. An example can be seen in two of their 1911 works—Picasso's *The Accordionist* and Braque's *Man with a Guitar*. Not only do the two works dramatically resemble one another in composition, the coloring used by both artists is quite similar. For Picasso, "this was to be his farthest foray into abstraction."[45]

Their partnership lasted through two phases of cubism—analytical, from 1909 to 1912 and synthetic, from 1912 to 1914. As early as 1911, their cubist works were almost completely

PABLO PICASSO'S LEGACY

CARRYING ON SPAIN'S ARTISTIC HERITAGE

Nearly 35 year after his death, the world remembers Pablo Picasso as one of the most prolific and ingenious artists of the twentieth century. Many, however, fail to note the important role Picasso's national heritage had on his art, as well as his life. He was a man wholly Spanish; one who considered himself the next great painter of Spanish descent.

This view of himself—that he was not only an artist, but a Spanish artist—continued to impact his art until his death.

Much of his art—including his subject matter and his stylistic approach—was the result of his Hispanic heritage. Picasso was consciously aware as he painted, sculpted, and drew that he often approached his work with the eye of a Spaniard. It was not that his subjects were related to Spain—such as bullfights, Mediterranean beaches, tile-roofed villas—or simply Spanish people. Rather, he manifested his Hispanic view of the world through a variety of other choices he made in his work as an artist:

> Picasso's. . .use of the monochromatic browns and ochers peculiar to the Spanish landscape, his love of the grotesque, his concern with the real even when painting at his most obscure—all these are indisputably in the tradition of Spanish painting. Despite the fact that he . . . lived in France since 1904, Picasso . . . remained thoroughly Spanish, both in his work and in his moods of *sol y sombra*—sun and shade.*

Those who were close to Picasso during his life understood the continuing influence that Picasso's love of Spain and all things Spanish had on him. One associate even noted how "when he speaks Spanish, his whole manner lightens, and his gestures quicken."**

Everywhere in his art, Picasso relied on his Hispanic background for

abstract. In 1914, the two men went their separate artistic ways. By then, their experiment with cubism "threatened to become a sterile exercise."[46] They both altered their style by

(*continued on page 54*)

inspiration. He also maintained an appreciation for the heritage of his people. Throughout his entire artistic career, Picasso was inspired by earlier Spanish artists, especially the great masters, including El Greco, Velázquez, Zurburan, Delacroix, and others. He studied their works, regularly returning to their paintings and using them as springboards for his own interpretations. As previously stated, he painted 15 canvases modeled after Delacroix's painting *Women of Algiers*. Velázquez's *Las Meninas* served as Picasso's inspiration to paint 44 of his own renditions. He never forgot the techniques employed by the masters, and he saw himself as the artistic extension of Spanish painting.

He also drew on other Spanish sources in his art. In his famous painting *Portrait of Gertrude Stein* (1906), Picasso may have used ancient Spanish sculpture, some carved by early Iberians who lived before the invasions of the Carthaginians and Romans, as models for Stein's face. His study of primitive medieval Spanish painting also impacted his works: Some thirteenth-century Catalan frescoes were used by Picasso in creating works such as *Woman in Yellow* (1907). These influences all originated from Spain and provided direction for Picasso's art.

Even in his later years, perhaps then more than at any other time in his life, Picasso never doubted the myriad ways his Hispanic heritage had impacted his art, as well as his view of the world. From his villa at Mougins, perched on a hill near Cannes on the French Riviera, he lived as close to Spain as his political views would allow. But, even in his self-imposed exile from his homeland, Picasso continually emphasized the one aspect of himself that was immutable: his Spanish heritage. Any time he opened his doors and allowed strangers to enter his world, he was always "the quintessential Spanish host, wholly absorbed in the comfort of his guest."***

   * Lael Wertenbaker, *The World of Picasso, 1881–1973* (Amsterdam: Time-Life Books, 1984), 10–11.
  ** Ibid., 11.
 *** Ibid., 8.

PICASSO'S "WIFE": GEORGES BRAQUE

Pablo Picasso was working to recreate the artistic world through cubism, but he was not alone in launching this avant-garde painting style. Georges Braque, another innovative painter in Picasso's inner circle of revolutionary artists, was also successful with this genre.

Braque, the son of a Le Havre house painter, rode into Paris on his bicycle in 1900, to be apprenticed to another house painter. He had other talents, however. He was soon drawn into the Parisian art world and began exhibiting with the fauvists. Unlike other Parisian artists of the early twentieth century, Braque never experienced poverty. His paintings were immediately popular, and in 1907, he sold all six of his works at his first exhibition. A fellow artist once spoke of Braque: "[He] always had a beefsteak in his stomach and some money in his pocket."*

That same year, when he saw Picasso's painting *Les Demoiselles D'Avignon*, he criticized the work. He soon set out to create a cubist painting of his own "in which he borrowed Picasso's idea of simultaneously showing the nude's face and back."** Like Picasso, Braque was influenced by Paul Cézanne (who died in 1906), and he created cubist landscapes after Cézanne, even before Picasso painted his *Houses on a Hill.* Braque presented these landscapes for public viewing in the fall of 1908, but they were met with a great deal of criticism and derision. Unfazed, Braque never stopped painting in the cubist style.

By 1909, Picasso and Braque, convinced that cubism was to become the artistic style of the future, formed a partnership with the intention of convincing the art world of the importance of cubism. The two men became so closely tied to one another that Braque compared themselves to "two rock climbers roped together."*** For Picasso, their friendship was equally important. He began referring to Braque as "his wife." When their artistic alliance drifted apart, he spoke of his former partner as "my ex-wife."† They were, of course, a peculiar pair. Their differences were marked. Picasso was outgoing with women; Braque was a shy man. Braque was strikingly handsome; Picasso often had a dark, foreboding appearance. Braque was quiet by nature; Picasso was volatile and emotional. Braque noted: "Picasso is Spanish and I am French. As everyone knows, that means a lot of differences, but during those years the differences did not count."††

The two men pushed their differences aside in support of cubism. Remembering 30 years later, Picasso recalled of their collaboration: "Just imagine almost every evening I went to Braque's studio or he came to mine. Each of us had to see what the other had done during the day. We criticized each other's work. A canvas wasn't finished unless both of us felt it was."††† The two men worked so closely together, that, since many of their early cubist paintings were never signed, "at the height of their relationship in 1911, it is difficult for the non-expert to distinguish the paintings of one from the other."‡

Whatever Braque might have owed Picasso through their years of collaboration, Picasso may have changed his French friend's life in another important way. Picasso once introduced Braque to a young woman, Marcelle Lapre, who soon became the French painter's model. In 1912, the two wed and enjoyed a happy marriage that lasted for more than 50 years, until Braque's death in 1963.

  * Lael Wertenbaker, *The World of Picasso, 1881–1973* (Amsterdam: Time-Life Books, 1984), 56.
 ** Ibid.
*** Andrew Brighton and Andrzej Klimowski, *Introducing Picasso* (New York: Totem, 1996), 60.
  † Wertenbaker, *The World of Picasso*, 58.
 †† Ibid.
††† Ibid.
  ‡ Brighton and Klimowski, 60.

(*continued from page 51*)

incorporating more realistic elements into their cubist compositions. They developed a new technique called *collage*, "where they incorporated everyday materials into their paintings,"[47] including sheet music, bottle labels, newspaper pages, and other items. The result was a blend of mediums, three-dimensional items, and even scrap materials, which created a cubist work that was both painting and sculpture. One such Picasso work is his *Still Life with Chair Caning* (1912), which includes an oil cloth painted to resemble chair caning, creating an optical illusion and blurring the line between reality and illusion. (This artistic device, of attempting to trick viewers into thinking they see something that is not truly being depicted, is referred to as *trompe l'oeil*, which translates as "deception of the eye.") Picasso included further innovation by framing his oval painting with a piece of rope. Fortunately, Picasso's cubist works found a market. By 1912, his primary patron was Daniel-Henry Kahnweiler. That year, Kahnweiler signed an exclusive contract with both Picasso and Braque to buy their cubist works, which he sold to a small number of elite buyers. When their paintings sold, however, Picasso's works often went for three or four times as much as Braque's.

LIFE CHANGES FOR PICASSO

During these years of artistic experimentation, Picasso also experienced significant changes in his personal life. In the fall of 1909, he and Fernande, along with their pet Siamese cat, moved to a spacious, luxury Parisian apartment at 11 Boulevard de Clichy near the Place Pigalle. The move from the bohemian world of the Bateau-Lavoir to an upscale neighborhood was dramatic. When moving men unloaded the couple's worn-out furniture into their new apartment, along with a great stack of painted canvases, they "thought the young couple must have drawn a lucky number in the National Lottery."[48] The move, however, was actually about Picasso's increasing fame and newfound prosperity. He was quite famous, not only in Spain and France, but also in Germany and even in the United States. (The first time a Picasso painting was exhibited publicly in the United States was in 1911 at the Photo Secession Gallery, in New York City. His cubist work was very well received at the great Armory Show in 1913, where his bronze bust, *Head of a Woman* [1909], was displayed.)

Picasso was at the center of the Parisian art world. Every Saturday, he and Fernande visited the Steins, and Matisse was always present. Between the two artists, "they were both among the most honored guests."[49] His cubist circle was widening, with such artists as André Derain taking up the new style, along with two new converts: Juan Gris, a fellow Spaniard from Madrid, and Fernand Léger, a Norman, like Braque.

As Picasso and Fernande moved up in the world, though, their relationship began to deteriorate. In their poverty, the two had remained faithful companions, but fame and fortune changed everything. As he collaborated closely with Braque, Picasso was distancing himself from Fernande. At night, he began to frequent the cafés of Montmartre, leaving her at home. They fought, as they always had, but the spark of passion between them had disappeared. Then, one spring night in 1912, Fernande left Picasso, leaving their apartment with "11 francs in her pocket and 40 bottles of perfume in her arms."[50] Their relationship had come to an end.

Although Picasso had loved Fernande, he had tired of her, as well. He wrote years later: "Her beauty held me, but I could not stand any of her little ways."[51] As for Picasso, he wasted no time in replacing Fernande. He had already begun flirting with a friend of Fernande's, Marcelle Humbert, who had recently been the mistress of another artist. In contrast to Fernande's fiery spirit, Marcelle was more quiet and sedate. Picasso called her "Eva," "an illusion to her becoming the first woman in his affection."[52] Picasso painted several "realistic" portraits of Fernande, but there were none of Eva. Unfortunately, he was in his cubist phase, so no portraits of her exist that present her realistically. During the years of their relationship, however, Picasso scribbled "J'aime Eva"—"I love Eva"—on several of his cubist paintings, like a schoolboy carving his girlfriend's initials on a tree. He also referred to her by inscribing cubist paintings with "MA JOLIE," a line from a popular song of the day—"My Joy"—which was a veiled tribute to his new love, "Eva."

Over the following two years, Picasso experienced some of his greatest joys and his most difficult tragedies. He was in his early 30s, yet his artistic style was still changing. During the summer of 1912, he and Marcelle moved to a house in southern France, in the sleepy town of Sorgues sur Ouvèze, 6 miles north of Avignon. Here the new couple found quiet and solitude. Braque and his new wife, also named Marcelle, moved nearby. Picasso's art gained a new energy. His cubist style was moving toward collage. In their rented house, Picasso drew sketches on its bare, whitewashed walls. When he left the house, his landlord charged him 50 francs to pay for repainting the walls. "What a fool," Picasso noted years later. "He could have sold the whole wall for a fortune if he had only had the sense to leave it."[53]

These months were pleasant and productive for Picasso, but by fall, he and Marcelle moved back to Paris, to a new studio in Montparnasse, along the Left Bank of the Seine River. This was a return into the new heart of the modern art world, as well as the intellectual center of Paris. Nearby were grand cafés, such as Le Dome and La Coupole, where Picasso met with his artistic colleagues. Cubism was becoming widely accepted, and a group of cubists called the "Golden Section" was attempting to redefine and restrict the artistic style by using mathematical formulas. Picasso and Braque were not pleased with this turn in the movement, and Braque later noted his feelings: "They started to lay down the law about how Cubism is like this and not like that and so on. I was hardly a man to start painting Braques in accordance with their rules."[54] Ultimately, the Golden Section died out quickly as a branch of cubism, but Picasso, Braque, Gris, and others in the circle of artists continued to experiment with the style. In

1912, Picasso created his three-dimensional cubist experiment *Guitar*, a collage of cardboard, paper, canvas, and string. The following year, he made an assemblage titled *Guitar and Bottle of Bass*, which was both painting and sculpture, cobbled together out of wood, paper, charcoal, and nails applied to a slab of wood. In creating such works, Picasso was attempting a type of collage that was more complex. It was a style he would abandon by 1915.

These two years, from 1912 to 1914, were, for Picasso, exciting, experimental, and rewarding. They would count as among the happiest of his life. All did not remain satisfactory, however. Picasso's father died late in 1913. Then, in August of the following year, war broke out across Europe. The call for troops went out immediately, which brought an end to Picasso's favorite circle of friends. Some left France for neutral Switzerland. Braque and Derain received their enlistment call while vacationing at Avignon with Picasso. Years later, Picasso remembered sadly: "I took them to the station at Avignon, and I never found them again."[55] Suddenly, death and war were unraveling Picasso's world.

5

New Movements

The war that began in Europe in the summer of 1914 would last until the fall of 1918. It would be a devastating conflict, the first modern war in history, with its tanks, planes, poison gas, stalemated trench warfare, and, its most deadly weapon, the machine gun. Although most of Europe would be pulled into the war, the predominant combatants were Great Britain, France, and Russia, which were opposed by Germany, Austria, and the Ottoman Empire (modern-day Turkey). Italy would join the Allies in 1915, and the United States came into the war as an ally in 1917. Millions of men would die in battles that stretched along the Western Front of rural France and Belgium. Before it was over, nearly an entire generation of young European men would be killed.

As war swept across Europe, Picasso faced personal struggles. His circle of friends was nearly depleted. The war was everywhere. (His close friend Braque would return from the war after having suffered serious wounds.) Even though the Spanish painter tried to ignore the ever-expanding conflict, it was impossible. Unlike his French friends, Picasso did not have to serve in the military, because Spain was not a combatant in the conflict. France was invaded, and the front was only 75 miles outside Paris. There was talk in the streets of Paris that the Germans might reach the city. Paris was "a changed city, robbed of its gaiety and anxiously watching the approach of the German armies."[56] As Picasso watched French gun carriages rolling down the streets of Paris, he noted how similar their bold, irregular camouflage patterns resembled cubism. "We did that!"[57] he told Gertrude Stein.

Perhaps most devastating to Picasso was the death of his loved one, Marcelle. She had fallen ill in 1913, a few months after Picasso's father died. By the early winter of 1914, her condition worsened, and she was placed in a nursing home. The artist commuted between his lonely apartment in Montparnasse and the nursing home. Her decline was gradual, and Marcelle died during the winter of 1915–1916, possibly from tuberculosis or cancer. The funeral was small; only seven or eight of Picasso's friends attended. Juan Gris was there, and he described the burial as "a very sad affair," to which he added, "Picasso is rather upset by it."[58] Soon, Picasso wrote to Gertrude Stein: "My poor Eva is dead . . . a great sorrow to me . . . she has always been so good to me."[59]

Following her death, Picasso gave up their apartment in Montparnasse and moved into a small house in Montrouge, a Parisian suburb. He struggled with loneliness, so he commuted into the city, where he met with Gertrude Stein and other friends in the cafés of Montparnasse. Soon, he met Erik Satie, an avant-garde composer, 15 years Picasso's senior. In many ways, what Picasso was doing in the art world, Satie was making happen in the music world. He, like his fellow modern composers Claude Debussy and Maurice Ravel, was

writing musical scores without using bar lines and key signa-
tures. His works abandoned harmonies for fragmented
melodies, much like the developing jazz music in the United
States.

COSTUMES AND SCENERY

When Picasso and Satie met, the composer was busy writing
music that was to be directed by Sergei Diaghilev, the producer

MODERN ARCHITECTURE AND CUBISM

Just as cubism managed to redefine reality, World War I introduced a new reality to the people of Europe. The continent continued to become industrialized and cities grew in population.
European workers, many of whom had fought in the killing fields
of the Western Front, expected to see returns on their personal
sacrifice through better working conditions, trade unions, and
increased political involvement. Much of the old agriculture-
based past seemed outdated, and the new, postwar European
wanted to live in better housing, work in modern factories, and
otherwise enjoy a standard of living that included new schools
and hospitals, and other social services.

   With a mandate to design new urban spaces, an innovative
generation of architects created a new style of building interior
spaces called functionalism. Gone was much of the heavy and
massive decoration of early buildings with their overwrought
stone carvings and intricate decoration. The new architectural
order called for function first, form second. Every part of a
building's design was rooted in purpose. Walls were left plain,
interrupted only by large panes of glass that let light stream in.
Flat roofs provided space for gardens. The craftsmanship of early
Western architecture gave way to industrial methods of building.
In some respects, this new architecture was rooted in the same
theories as Picasso's cubism.

   Two of the most important European functionalism archi-

of the Russian Ballet. By 1917, Satie invited Picasso to come to Rome and meet Diaghilev. Picasso agreed, and he soon found himself designing the scenery and costumes for the ballet *Parade*, which had been written by the poet Jean Cocteau. Picasso and Cocteau became close friends.

While in Italy, Picasso abandoned much of his cubism and entered a new cycle of painting—works that would still bear his unique stylistic mark but would represent a distinct return

tects were the French Le Corbusier (his real name was Charles-Edouard Jeanneret) and a German, Walter Gropius. Also a painter and sculptor, Le Corbusier designed his buildings as a means of solving social problems—to improve the lives of people. Gropius was the founder of a modern architectural school, the Bauhaus, which he established in 1919 in the postwar Weimar Republic of his native Germany. Like Le Corbusier, Gropius also believed that architecture could reflect society's moral values and help improve the way people lived. (Among his staff of teachers were several important artists of the 1920s, including Vasily Kandinsky and Paul Klee.)

Both these modern elements—cubism and functionalism—came together in 1923 in Le Corbusier's design for the La Roche House. It was built as two homes—one for Le Corbusier's younger brother, Albert, and another to house the modern art collection of Raoul La Roche, a wealthy patron. The result was a functional "museum" with stark white interior walls, long lines of glass to light the interior, and openness to its uncluttered spaces. Le Corbusier designed the house-museum around La Roche's collection of modern paintings, observing his own rule: "Form follows function." The result was one of the first buildings of the twentieth century designed to create a harmony between modern architecture and modern art.

In 1917, Picasso's friend Erik Satie invited him to Italy to design scenery and costumes for the Russian ballet, which was performing in Rome. During his time with the Russian ballet, Picasso met a ballerina named Olga Koklova, whom he depicted in *Portrait of Olga in an Armchair*. Olga and Picasso married in 1918, and Olga gave birth to Picasso's first child, Paulo, in 1921.

to realism. Throughout Rome, as well as other Italian art centers, including Florence, the Spanish artist could study closely the High Renaissance art of such masters as Michelangelo and

Raphael. He also visited the ruins of Pompeii, where he admired the ancient Roman frescoes. Here, and across Italy, he found new inspiration.

The avant-garde remained the inspiration for his ballet costuming, however. Picasso's costumes were giant cubist works, but perhaps his most important contribution was the painting of the enormous stage curtain. Picasso did not paint it in the cubist style but instead returned to a stylized realism, a work that looked like a "giant circus poster."[60] When the ballet was first performed in Paris at the Théâtre du Châtelet, in May 1917, it nearly caused a riot. Put off by Satie's deafening and strange music, the Parisian audience was outraged. Even as the opening night audience hissed at the ballet, though, they applauded the Picasso curtain. Picasso would also design costumes and sets for other Diaghilev ballets. During these collaborations, he met Olga Koklova, a beautiful ballerina in Diaghilev's company and daughter of a colonel in the Imperial Russian Military. The Spanish painter was soon in love. Olga would replace Eva as Picasso's lover. By July 1918, Picasso and Olga married. They moved into an apartment on the Rue La Boetie, an affluent street near the Champs-Elysées.

Picasso had been revived again. For the moment, he was happy, his fame was growing, and he had all the money he could possibly want. As for Olga, she knew how to spend it. She created a comfortable world for them both:

> She decorated the apartment lavishly and in the latest fashion, with a living room all in white and a bedroom sporting a new fad, twin beds. Floor-length draperies hung at the windows and handsomely framed pictures hung on the walls: Cézannes, Renoirs, Corots and some of Picasso's Cubist paintings. Picasso rented a similar apartment on the floor above to use as a studio. There he kept to his Bohemian habits and usual clutter. But otherwise, under Olga's influence, he became notably bourgeois. He took to wearing tailored suits,

with a gold watch chain attached to his buttonhole. He groomed his hair meticulously and tucked a handkerchief into his breast pocket. He also uncomplainingly walked his wife's Russian wolfhounds.[61]

Just months after Picasso and Olga's wedding, the Great War ended. With millions of troops killed, the war left a psychological scar on the continent. The devastation of the war only rekindled a spirit of protest and challenge among artists, writers, and intellectuals, many of whom became cynical about the future and bitterly determined to redefine the moral and political landscape of Europe. Refusing to give lip service to the old status quo, art movements and other intellectual circles stepped up the pressure to reject conformity and societal standards, and to make way for twentieth-century ideas. Picasso would continue to redefine the century's art.

PICASSO'S NEWLY DIRECTED LIFE

For the next two years, Picasso and Olga lived an enviable life. They were wealthy, he was famous, and they mingled with high society, while the value of his paintings continued to increase. During those two years, Picasso designed stage sets. He also painted and continued to experiment, but he remained generally true to his return to realism. He painted Olga over and over and, with each painting, portrayed her in a different style. In a 1917 portrait, *Olga in an Armchair*, his future wife is painted in stark realism, with sedate colors to match her disposition. In the 1920 portrait *Woman Reading (Olga)*, she is depicted in a simpler, almost childlike style, which seems directly influenced by the work of a Greek-born, Italian painter of the period, Giorgio de Chirico.

In 1919, while working with the Russian Ballet on another production, Picasso visited London. He had set out for the city 20 years earlier but had wound up in Paris. Since the ballet was based on a nineteenth-century Spanish novel, *The Three-Cornered Hat*, his designs, including a new curtain, featured Spanish subjects. As for his curtain, it portrayed a bullfight. Gone were the exaggerated cubist costumes; instead, he designed them using patterns taken from traditional Spanish peasant wagons. When performed, the ballet was an overnight success. His days in London were fulfilling, and he and Olga were entertained from one corner of the city to another. Normalcy was returning to Picasso's world. The war was over, he was in love, and his star was continuing to rise. In 1921, he was overjoyed at the birth of his first child, a son named Paulo.

With the arrival of the 1920s, Picasso was again busying himself with experimentation in his art. He could paint anything he felt like, and his subjects ranged from bathers by the sea, to clowns, to his wife, Olga. Some of his paintings mirrored his studies of High Renaissance Italian art he had made a few years earlier. Among these mannerist paintings, *The Seated Woman* (1920), *Two Nude Women Seated* (1920), and *The Race* (1922) serve as prime examples. All three include women who are drawn in massive scale. In *The Race*, a pair of giantesses run along a seashore, hand-in-immense-hand. To the viewer, they are "so ponderous that their earthshaking footfalls seem almost audible [yet] the women nonetheless have the lithe mobility of ballet dancers."[62] Their faces, limbs, and extremities are grotesquely portrayed, heavy and inflated, but the subjects represent a new style of Picasso realism.

Despite this new postwar realism of Picasso's, he had not yet abandoned cubism. As a result, he produced one of his recognized career masterpieces, *Three Musicians*. (Picasso actually produced two versions of the painting at the same time, both with the same title.) He completed the work in the summer of 1921. The painting is a triumph of synthetic cubism, the second phase of cubism. Unlike analytical cubism, its figures are flat, brightly colored, and portrayed in a fractured but still interpretive realism. In both versions, the three figures fill the canvas. In one, a white-costumed Pierrot (a comic character) is shown playing a recorder; a harlequin strums a guitar; and a

During the early 1920s, Picasso returned to the second phase of cubism—synthetic cubism. The figures in *Three Musicians*, which Picasso painted in 1921, are flat, brightly colored, and portrayed in a fractured but still interpretive realism. Music was a favorite cubist theme and Picasso's subjects are equipped with a violin, a recorder, and a concertina.

dark-robed, singing monk holds sheet music in his lap. In both versions, the monk is depicted on the right, but the Pierrot and harlequin switch middle and left positions in each version. In the second version, the harlequin plays a violin, and the monk holds a concertina. In the first version, the shadow of a dog is included behind the Pierrot.

Although Picasso paints his three musicians in the realm of

realism, he creates them through a series of colored shapes, with no depth. The realism is not stark or naturalistic, but at least it is identifiable to the eye and conveys a comfort that his analytical cubist pieces, works that bordered on the abstract, could not. At the same time, each version of his *Three Musicians* is "a jigsaw puzzle of circles, triangles and rectangles."[63] The result is, in both versions of *Three Musicians*, that the canvases are whimsical and light, yet mysterious, as if the trio inhabits another spatial dimension. For the viewer, especially one who had been exposed to earlier cubist works that avoided any vestige of realism, this pair of similar compositions must have seemed like a breath of fresh air. They also reveal an amazing versatility in Picasso's art.

A New Love

Although Picasso's fame and fortune continued to grow, he was not content with his standing. Even as the Great Depression struck in 1929 and spread through the industrialized Western nations, Picasso never lacked for money. During the early 1930s, other artists began to face money problems and even financial crises. This was not true for Picasso, though—he was wealthy and had enough money to buy an eighteenth-century chateau located about 40 miles outside of Paris. The Château de Boisgeloup was immense: it included nearly two dozen rooms, a Gothic chapel, and a large pigeon loft. (Picasso had enjoyed pigeons as a child; they were a favorite of his father's.) Outbuildings provided the Spanish artist with space for studios, where he painted and created metal sculptures along with a sculptor-friend, Julio Gonzalez.

Even as he lived splendidly in a beautiful house, driving a fine car, and enjoying what money could buy, he was not satisfied. He had promised himself years earlier that he would "live like a poor man with a great deal of money."[64] Even as he clung to this romantic idea, though, his wife, Olga, would have none of it. Although she had posed for him earlier in their marriage many times, she was not really that interested in his art. She wanted to climb the social ladder. She wanted a life of proper convention. Olga, to Picasso, became domineering and demanding. She constantly tried to tame his independent spirit. Their marriage lasted until 1935—when Olga finally left Picasso, taking their son, Paulo, with her—but the Spanish painter had abandoned the marriage years earlier and had found love elsewhere.

His new object of passion was Marie-Therese Walter. Picasso met her in 1927, when he struck up a conversation with her outside a Parisian department store. She was just 17 years old and was so different from Olga. Marie-Therese was a large blonde, free-spirited and easy going, sensual and passive. They soon began a secret affair, and Picasso rented an apartment for her, one that was close to his own. Picasso could not keep Marie-Therese under wraps forever. By the winter of 1931, he was using her as a model.

Even as his marriage was disintegrating, Picasso dabbled in yet another artistic style. In 1925, he painted *The Three Dancers*, a work that did not abandon realism, but, as he had done in the past, used it "to rip the human body apart, dislocating arms, noses, breasts, mouths."[65] The painting does not appear to be the result of careful study and analysis that had provided the foundation of his cubist experiments. Instead, he seems intent on creating a new, nightmarish reality centered in a troubled psyche. Perhaps he was transferring the pain of his failing marriage to the canvas. Other, similar works, based on disfigured displays of the female body followed, including his *Woman in an Armchair* (1929); *Seated Bather* (1930), with its shades of sand and water; and *Figure in a Red Chair* (1932), which depicts the female form as a disjointed set of circles, orbs, scrolling flat surfaces, clumsy appendages, and cannonball breasts.

That same year, he produced another of his acknowledged masterpieces of style, *Girl Before a Mirror*. Whereas his female portraits in the year just prior had featured women he practically dissected with an artistic violence, this painting represents a different treatment of its female subject. He is still dabbling with cubism, and a frenetic mixture of colors—brilliant reds, yellows, greens, shades of orange, and violets—brings the portrait of Marie-Therese to life. The dual images are disturbing, though, especially the woman's reflection in the cheval glass (full-length mirror). The image in the glass, while reminiscent of the woman, is not a direct, physical reflection. Perhaps Picasso is toying with the psychological, depicting images that reveal a split personality. The image of the girl looking in the mirror appears "innocent and childlike,"[66] whereas her reflection looks older, even darker, perhaps signifying old age or some psychological alter ego. Perhaps Picasso is presenting his mistress both as an attractive young woman and as a temptress who has drawn him away from his wife. Art historians continue to debate.

The End of a Marriage

By 1935, Picasso's personal life reached a new level of complication. Marie-Therese was pregnant. Although Olga left Picasso that same year, they never legally divorced. At that time, the Spanish government did not recognize divorce, and Picasso would have had to give up his Spanish citizenship to divorce Olga. The following year, Marie-Therese gave birth to a daughter, Maya. She and her daughter lived across the city, and Picasso visited his daughter frequently. Even in Olga's absence, Picasso and Marie-Therese did not remain a couple. He was, after all, technically, still a married man, and he was a lonely man, as well. An old friend, Jaime Sabartés, who came to Paris to help Picasso recover from his emotional losses, became his constant companion. He remained Picasso's personal secretary for the rest of his life.

Picasso remained dispirited, and he struggled to produce any artwork at all. He grew cranky with his friends, and his temper was more violent than ever before. Sabartés recalled how Picasso "refused to set foot in his studio. The mere sight of his pictures and drawings exasperated him, for every one of them recalled something of his recent past and every memory was an unhappy one."[67] According to Gertrude Stein, her Spanish friend "ceased to paint in 1935. In fact, he ceased to paint during two years and he neither painted nor drew . . . It was very curious."[68] Despite the observations of his friends, Picasso did paint between 1935 and 1937. Most of his works were portraits of Marie-Therese. However, he did not sell these paintings and kept them from the public eye for years.

Despite his depression and loneliness, Picasso's professional career continued to gain momentum. He collaborated with a surrealist poet, Paul Éluard, whom he had met shortly after World War I. Picasso provided the illustrations for a book of surrealist verse published in 1936. That same year, a group of young Spanish artists and poets—the Friends of the Arts—organized a retrospective exhibit of Picasso's artwork in Barcelona. Although Picasso did not attend the exhibit, he did send several paintings and other works to be included along with works provided by art galleries and dealers. His friend Éluard attended in his place and presented a lecture. Three other Picasso exhibits were held in Paris in 1936 to honor the 55-year-old Spanish painter, including one at the Rosenberg Gallery, next to Picasso's apartment. Many art admirers who attended the Rosenberg exhibit tried to get a glimpse of Picasso in and around his apartment. Some gawkers found "that it was easy to catch sight of him through his bathroom window."[69]

That summer, Picasso vacationed in Juan-les-Pins on the French Riviera, taking along Marie-Therese, who was several months pregnant with their daughter Maya. After a couple of months, they returned to Paris, where Picasso went to work on a set of engravings for a book on natural history. Before the summer was over, he returned to the Riviera, this time to the town of Mougins. His companions were Éluard and his wife, but he left Marie-Therese behind. During an outdoor luncheon in neighboring St. Tropez, the middle-aged Picasso spotted a black-haired beauty named Dora Maar. Although Yugoslavian, she had grown up in Argentina, so she could speak Spanish. Picasso introduced himself, he took a walk with her after lunch, and, before the day was over, he had convinced her to come to Mougins with him. This green-eyed woman soon became his lover and his model for the next ten years.

War and Peace

Once again, Picasso had rebounded from the loss of a lover (or wife, in the case of Olga) and found himself a new female companion. Whatever depression he had been struggling with was gone. His new love was of aristocratic birth, intelligent, a professional photographer, outgoing, and sensually appealing to the Spanish artist. She was an admirer of modern art and had personally moved for years within a circle of surrealist painters. In more than one way, Dora spoke Picasso's language. Their relationship would last through World War II. Yet, even with his new relationship with Dora, Picasso did not end his relationship with Marie-Therese. She was, after all, the mother of his daughter. In fact, he continued to use her as a model in 1937, painting several experimental and varied portraits of her.

Picasso's personal life was getting back on track, but dark events were swirling around him—events he could not ignore. Great political and military movements were afoot across Europe by the 1930s, many of them geared for war and a new extremism. The German Fascist leader Adolf Hitler rose to power in 1933 and took control of the fledging Weimar Republic, installing his National Socialist Party (the Nazis) as the controlling force. In Italy, another Fascist dictator, Benito Mussolini, had already seized the helm of his country's government, and in Picasso's native Spain, political turmoil would erupt into civil war. The year was 1936. In 1931, the Spanish people had thrown off hundreds of years of aristocratic rule and established a shaky democracy in its place, the Second Republic. This government presided over a country that was backward compared to other European states; its people generally poor, and its industrial system limited. The Spain of the early 1930s was dominated by aristocratic landowners, industrialists, the Catholic Church, and its military. With the government in need of reform, political extremists challenged its power, typically calling for a strong centralized government and a greater level of local independence. Each political group—Communists, Socialists, Fascists—hoped to weaken the Republican government and gain power.

In the early spring of 1936, Spanish elections resulted in the establishment of a coalition government that included many Republicans, as well as Communists and Socialists. Despite some reform attempts, the new government was not popular. By July, a band of renegade army officers revolted against the Popular Front. Three months later, the rebel army, led by General Francisco Franco, laid siege to the government in Madrid. On October 1, Franco declared himself the head of state. Soon, he installed a military dictatorship. The fighting did not stop, however, and Spain found itself plunged into civil war, pitting Franco's Fascist followers against the Republicans. The conflict was further fueled when Nazi Germany and Fascist Italy supported Franco, while the Stalin-led Communist government of the Soviet Union sided with the Republicans. Both Franco and the Republicans received military support from these powerful, extremist leaders.

As for Picasso, while he was not, by nature, a political creature, he sided with the Republicans. He became a major benefactor on behalf of Spanish relief programs. He sold paintings he had been keeping for years and gave the money to those who had been dispossessed by the war. He also contributed money from his personal fortune. One Spanish official estimated that Picasso gave 400,000 francs in direct relief to provide food for starving Spaniards, as well as money to support political figures and Spanish intellectuals. He was not alone in his support of the Republicans. Most Spanish artists, writers, and intellectuals did not want Franco to come to power, and they, too, eagerly contributed to the Republican cause.

The Friends of the Arts convinced the Republican government to name Picasso the director *in absentia* of Spain's greatest museum, the Prado, located in war-torn Madrid. They hoped to use Picasso's international fame and prestige to draw world sympathy to their political plight. He accepted the offer, but the conflict between Franco's forces and the Republican government turned Madrid into a battleground. Paintings were removed from the Prado, even Picasso's. Picasso observed, "So I am director of an empty museum."[70] Despite greatly assisting the Republican cause, though, his greatest contribution would be made the following year, in 1937.

THE HORRORS OF WAR

Early in 1937, Picasso vented his anti-Franco sentiment by creating a set of copper plate etchings and a critical poem of the Spanish Fascist. In his art, he portrayed Franco as "a grotesque creature like a cancerous, hairy turnip, wearing a crown and grinning evilly from a mouth in its middle."[71] In his poetry, Picasso expressed raw emotion at the atrocities that were being committed by Franco's forces on his fellow countrymen: "Cries of children cries of women cries of birds cries of flowers cries of timbers and of stones cries of bricks cries of

Picasso's most famous work, *Guernica*, reflects his outrage over the bombings carried out by the German Luftwaffe in 1937 on the painting's namesake—the Spanish town of Guernica. The cubist work, which is done in white, black, and grays, presents a message of tragedy, destruction, and hopelessness; Picasso's subjects' eyes, limbs, ears, and faces are fragmented and out of alignment with nature.

furniture of beds of chairs of curtains of pots of cats and of papers."[72] He titled the combined work, *The Dream and Lie of Franco*. But he would produce greater anti-Franco art. Following the attack against the defenseless Basque town of Guernica, Picasso was outraged and inspired to paint his giant mural in protest. The story of the attack revealed the cold-blooded planning that had taken place by Nazi officials against the Basque community:

> They attacked at the busiest hour of a market day; the streets were jammed with townspeople and peasants in from the countryside. Never before in modern war had noncombatants been slaughtered in such numbers, and by such means. Worse still, Guernica had no strategic value for Franco's armies, but it had a poignant meaning for 600,000 Basques: from the early Middle Ages onward, it had been a kind of capital for the

Basques, symbolizing their independent spirit and democratic ideals.[73]

Analyzing Picasso's *Guernica*

On the surface, as with so much of Picasso's art, *Guernica*'s composition is frenetic but not especially complicated. He continues to rely on the basic element of cubism, depicting his victims of war in a distorted realism. The eyes, limbs, ears, and faces of his subjects are fragmented and out of alignment with nature. At the center of the work is a horse, wounded by war, and the eye moves to its frightened head. Beneath its hooves lies a fallen warrior, holding the broken hilt of a sword. Four women occupy the canvas. On the far left, a mother wails to the heavens, while holding her baby who appears dead; the only being in the painting depicted without an open mouth. The viewer is reminded of Picasso's anti-Franco poetry: "Cries of children cries of women."

At the painting's right, a trio of women reveal a victim's range of emotion as their faces register everything from shock to horror. One is escaping her burning house, her own clothing on fire. Another flees in a panic. The third, depicted with only a head and an arm, holds a lamp, which offers little illumination. There is another light, above the horse's head, a symbolic sun "shaped like an eye with an electric bulb for a pupil."[74] The symbols are concrete; the impact is hard hitting. Only one other being is present, at the far left—a bull. Picasso later explained the symbolism of both the bull and the horse: "The Bull is not fascism, but it is brutality and darkness . . . The horse represents the people."[75] The message of the work is so potent that Picasso easily achieves his specific goal: "a monumental protest against darkness and brutality."[76]

To add to the stark portrayal of war, its victims, and its horrors, Picasso made the decision early on not to use color but to simply portray the entire work in white, black, and grays. The symbolism is, then, complete. The work presents tragedy, destruction, and hopelessness. Only a faint impression of a flower at the bottom center of the painting, near the fallen defender's broken sword, offers even a faint sense of hope that life goes on even in the aftermath of war's destruction. So complete and universal are Picasso's themes in *Guernica* that the painting shouts across all political and social lines. By starkly depicting the violent excesses of war, "Picasso's personal protest at a comparatively small incident in his own country afterwards acquired a world-wide significance."[77]

By July 12, Picasso's painting was on display in the Spanish Pavilion of the Paris International Exhibition. As the Fascist attack on Guernica had produced a firestorm of international protest, so Picasso's large mural created its own whirlwind of controversy. He was criticized by extremists on both the left and right. Supporters of Franco were, naturally, not pleased with the work. Republicans were disappointed that Picasso's vision was so simplistic and nonspecific. To them, he had not directly criticized the Fascists. His portrayal seemed vague. He had not used his paints and brushes to call the victims of Fascist aggression to take up arms of their own. As for the art critics, some spoke against the work, saying that it lacked originality. The British critic Herbert Read defended Picasso, however: "Picasso's symbols are banal like the symbols of Homer, Dante, Cervantes."[78]

After the Paris International Exhibition closed, Picasso's great antiwar painting was sent out on tour: it was exhibited in London and other capitals of Europe, and finally in New York City. Picasso sent all the profits from these traveling exhibitions to help support the Republican defense of Spain. The Spanish Civil War finally came to an end, though, with the surrender of the Republican government in Madrid on March 28, 1939. After three years of bloody conflict, Franco's Fascists took full power, and 750,000 people were dead.

THE WAR YEARS

To Picasso, the destruction of the town of Guernica represented extreme brutality administered by a destructive aggressor.

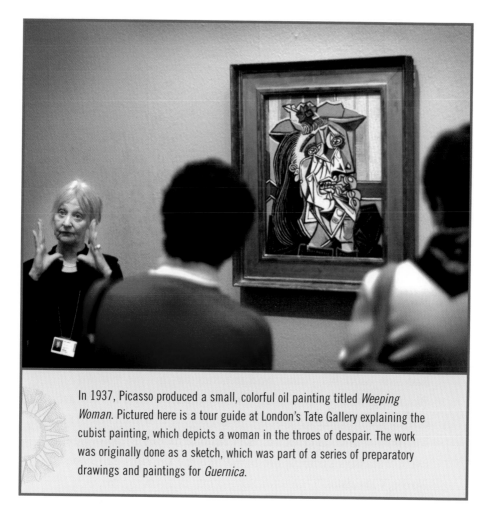

In 1937, Picasso produced a small, colorful oil painting titled *Weeping Woman*. Pictured here is a tour guide at London's Tate Gallery explaining the cubist painting, which depicts a woman in the throes of despair. The work was originally done as a sketch, which was part of a series of preparatory drawings and paintings for *Guernica*.

In the years that followed 1937, however, Europe, as well as much of the rest of the world, was plunged into an all-encompassing war, extending the plight of Basque victims to millions internationally. World War II began in earnest in the fall of 1939, and the war in Europe did not end until Mussolini's Fascists and Hitler's Nazis were utterly defeated. Against the backdrop of war, Picasso continued to work and gain further fame. He spent the summers of 1937 and 1938 on the Riviera. Dora posed for multiple portraits, and their lives were as luxurious as ever. Picasso owned an expensive car, a Hispano-Suiza, and Dora a sleek Afghan hound. But as Hitler became more aggressive and the conflict expanded in Europe, the war never completely left Picasso's mind. Late in 1937, he produced a small oil painting, *Weeping Woman*; yet another colorful, cubist composition. This creation was of a woman in the throes of despair, a brilliant work reminiscent of the horror-stricken victims of his *Guernica*.

On September 1, Nazi armies invaded Poland and, on September 3, France and Great Britain declared war on Germany. Picasso and Dora rushed back to Paris. Three days later, they left the capital for the port city of Royan, where they rented rooms, uncertain of the future of the City of Light. They stayed in Royan until August 1940. By then, German troops had marched across Western Europe, invaded France's defenses along the Maginot Line, and had reached Paris itself. Even as the Germans occupied the city, Picasso did not flee but returned to Paris and moved into the Rue Des Grans-Augustins, the aristocratic house where he had created *Guernica*. He was offered sanctuary in Mexico and the United States, but Picasso chose to remain in Paris, despite German control. There he remained through four years of German occupation.

During those years, poet Max Jacob, his old Jewish friend of more than 40 years, was arrested by the German secret police, the Gestapo. Jacob had many years earlier converted to Catholicism (Picasso had attended his baptism) and was living in a monastery. With his arrest, he was shipped to a concentration camp in 1944, where he died just months before the liberation of Paris. When his body was returned to Paris, Picasso chose to attend his old friend's funeral, even though he risked being reprimanded by German authorities. Other friends of Jacob stayed away.

Picasso could get away with taking such bold chances. He was, after all, Picasso, one of the most famous artists in Europe. There were times when his fame came in handy with the Germans. When he was found eating at black-market restaurants in Paris, German officials turned a blind eye. Other actions earned him the disfavor of the occupying Germans, however. According to Arno Breker, one of Hitler's favorite German sculptors, he had to intervene on Picasso's behalf when German officials caught the Spanish painter attempting to smuggle currency out of France.

From time to time, German officials, aware of his fame, attempted to offer Picasso special favors to gain his support and collaboration, but he always refused. He struggled through shortages of food and fuel, and spent cold winters painting while wearing heavy clothing and gloves with the fingers cut out of them.

His art from this time period included paintings and a

PICASSO AND THE GERMAN OCCUPATION

The war years took their toll on Picasso, who turned 60 in 1941. The German authorities would not allow him to exhibit his works—Hitler had decided they were too "degenerate." He continued to work as best he could, but he was constantly short on supplies. Perhaps inspired to find new materials for his art, he once created a simple sculpture from an unlikely source: He made bas-relief sculptures using cardboard and cigarette boxes. He fashioned a bird out of a broken piece of a toddler's scooter. While taking a walk one day in 1943, he found a discarded bicycle. He took the handlebars and metal bike seat home with him and soon fashioned them into the likeness of a bull, the tapered seat serving as the head and the handlebars reminiscent of a pair of horns.

There were other shortages, as well, including food and fuel. Because of his fame, the German ambassador in Paris, Otto Abetz, offered him a supply of coal in exchange for his cooperation with the Third Reich. Picasso refused, claiming, "A Spaniard is never cold!"* His apartments and studio were often cold through the war, forcing him to work in heavy sweaters. During another visit from Abetz, the German official saw a

renewed interest in sculpture. He seems to have become obsessed with skulls, both human and animal. He produced his famous *Head of a Bull* (1943) from bicycle scraps, using the handlebars for horns and the seat for the bull's head. He paint- ed his *Still Life with Bull's Head* in 1939, and a similar work, *Still Life with Ox Skull*, in 1942. Both represent another varia- tion on his cubist theme. A 1944 sculpture, *Death's Head*, rep- resented a rotting, human skull. How much the war impacted such works is uncertain. It is likely that Picasso tried to con- tinue his creative efforts by avoiding such external distrac- tions. This was not always possible, however, as his *Death's*

photograph of Picasso's *Guernica*. "Ah Monsieur Picasso," he observed, "So it was you who did that?" Picasso coolly respond- ed: "No, it was you."**

As the German Occupation dragged from one year into the next, he created dozens of plaster sculptures. At first, they could not be cast, however, "because the Nazis had commandeered all metals, especially bronze . . . not to turn into cannon but to be recast as monuments to Hitler."*** When friends began to worry that the plasters might be lost or damaged if they were not cast, they worked out a plan. Aware of a secretly hidden supply of bronze, they began delivering one plaster at a time to a local foundry, hiding the work in a wheelbarrow filled with garbage. Once the plaster was cast in bronze, they would trundle it back to Picasso, in the same wheelbarrow, under the same garbage. All the time, their work went undetected, even under the scruti- nizing eye of German Gestapo security agents.

* Lael Wertenbaker, *The World of Picasso, 1881–1973* (Amsterdam: Time-Life Books, 1984), 130.
** Ibid.
*** Ibid., 130–131.

Head suggests. The work could easily be interpreted as a blatant metaphor for the horrors committed by Nazi Germany during the war.

By June 1944, Allied armies had landed on France's Normandy coast. The liberation of Paris seemed near. On August 24, fighting could be heard in the streets of the city, and "the whole of Paris was roused by the noise of sniping from the roofs and gunfire from the retreating German tanks."[79] Picasso soon found his studio in the middle of the raging street fighting. Nearby explosions rattled his studio windows. The old Spanish artist, heartened by the approaching Allied victory, continued working in his studio, where he loudly sang to cover up the sharp noises of fighting in the streets below. He was busy creating a sculpture, his own version of *The Triumph of Pan*, a light, joyful piece, symbolic of the retreat of German troops from the streets of Paris.

On August 25, the City of Light was free, the Germans gone, and the streets were filled with excited Parisians—men, women, and children crying for joy. Soon, Picasso's studio became besieged, but this time, by an army of friends and reporters, as well as curious Allied soldiers who knew of Picasso's fame:

Hardly had the rattle of automatic weapons ceased when friends serving with the Allied armies began to arrive. The news that had reached the outside world about Picasso had been scarce and unreliable. Even those who knew him only as a name were anxious to find out what had happened to him. It was a race to see who could find him first. . . . The first to climb the narrow winding staircase and reach the door of his studio was Lee Miller, who was at that time war correspondent for *Vogue*. With tears in his eyes, he welcomed her, astonished to see that the first Allied "soldier" he should meet was a woman. Every day more friends crowded in and news was eagerly exchanged about those who were absent or dead. Picasso's survival through the perils of war became a symbol of victory;

applied to him the word "liberation" was synonymous with his work and life.[80]

A revolving door of visitors, friends, and well-wishers continued to arrive at Picasso's apartment for days following the liberation. During the latter days of the war (the Germans would be defeated by the Allies by the following May), the old Spanish painter became a symbol of defiance; an aged artist who had stood against the Germans through dark Parisian days. To Picasso, his actions during the occupation had been necessary. He would explain years later: "This was not the moment for a creative man to throw in the sponge, accept defeat and stop work. There was nothing to do but go on working seriously and enthusiastically struggle to find food, calmly continue to see one's friends, and await freedom."[81] Freedom had come at last, and Picasso would witness not only the difficulties and privations of war, but yet another generation of modern art, to which he would make even more important contributions.

Painting Politics

With the liberation of Paris, Picasso once again enjoyed freedom. Old friends came to visit, and the outside world was reintroduced to the aging Spanish artist. The end of the long, German-driven nightmare that had fallen over Paris was over. Yet, even as the Allies drove the occupying Germans from the streets of Paris, Parisians, including Picasso, learned of the atrocities committed in Nazi concentration camps. News began to reach the city that millions of people, many of them Jews, had been rounded up and shipped to work and death camps. In response, Picasso produced another antiwar work of art, *Charnel House* (1944–1945). The piece is reminiscent of his *Guernica*, painted in black, white, and grays. It features a trio of victims—a man, woman, and child— lying dead, perhaps starved to death. To add to the grim nature of the painting, the corpses are shown next to a table spread with food. Unable or unwilling to wage war with a gun, Picasso chose to fight in his own way, later describing his intent: "Painting . . . is an instrument of war," with which one may battle "brutality and darkness."[82]

He became more connected than ever with public service, driven by his conscience to participate in the rebuilding of Europe in the aftermath of a devastating war. He served on a committee of artists, selected by the new provisional president of France, General Charles de Gaulle, which would authorize works depicting the war. In October 1944, after the liberation of Paris, Picasso took a bold, anti-Fascist step and joined the Partie Communiste Francais (PCF), the French Communist Party. At that time, Communism was seen by many in France as the best resistance movement against Nazi Fascism. Picasso joined the organization for just that reason. He explained: "What I joined at the end of the war was a party which had opposed Franco, whose members had played a leading role in the French resistance, and which promised social justice and peace."[83] In addition, Fascism in Spain had taken root. Franco was still in power at the end of World War II, and he would remain in power for another 30 years, maintaining his Fascist power base until two years after Picasso's death in 1973. When Franco came to power in Picasso's homeland, the Spanish artist vowed he would not set foot in Spain as long as Franco lived and ruled.

Six weeks after the liberation, in an attempt to reassert their new freedom, a grand exhibition of artwork, called the "Salon de la Liberation," was organized by Parisians. Although Picasso did not usually display his works with those of other artists at such exhibitions, he agreed to send five sculptures and more than 70 paintings. Most of them had been completed during the war.

ANOTHER RELATIONSHIP

The war had changed much for Pablo Picasso, including his personal life. He had continued his relationship with Dora Maar through much of the war, but he had also continued to visit Marie-Therese and their daughter. In fact, he was living

Yugoslavian-born photographer and artist Dora Maar, pictured here in 1955 with one of her paintings, was Picasso's mistress from 1936 to 1943. Maar documented the painting of *Guernica* through a series of photographs, many of which were purchased by the French government in 1998 for the Musée Picasso in Paris.

with them during the street fighting in Paris in the summer of 1944. Another woman was becoming a part of Pablo Picasso's life, however. In 1943, he met Françoise Gilot, a painter in her early 20s. As with so many of Picasso's love interests, she was young, beautiful, and intelligent. She was also an artist. In her memoirs, published 20 years later, she described her personal introduction to the great Spanish artist, whose work she had come to admire: "I met Pablo Picasso in May 1943, during the

German Occupation of France. I was twenty-one and I felt already that painting was my whole life."[84] She met him at a dinner party hosted by a mutual friend. Although Dora Maar was also present in the room, Picasso seemed to take notice of Françoise and invited her and a female companion to visit him. When Françoise's friend told Picasso they were both painters, he immediately responded, telling them: "You must come to my studio and see some of *my* paintings."[85] The next day, the two young girls were given a tour of Picasso's studio. During the days that followed, Françoise and Picasso became lovers, and Françoise found herself living a life that, in her words, "seemed miraculous."[86] She was drawn to Picasso: "I knew that here was something larger than life, something to match myself against. [He] was a challenge I could not turn down."[87] She would remain his companion for the next ten years.

Even as Picasso began to nurture a relationship with Françoise, he remained with Dora Maar. Their personal relationship was deteriorating quickly, and they began to argue constantly. Dora finally went insane in 1944, "possibly provoked by Picasso's treatment of her."[88] He continued his relationship with Françoise, and they began living together in the spring of 1946. The aged painter and the young artist moved to Antibes, a French Riviera resort town between Nice and Cannes. There, a local museum curator let Picasso use several rooms in the Grimaldi Palace as a studio. These were happy months for Picasso and Françoise. The following year, she gave birth to their first child, a boy they named Claude: "a black-eyed infant who strongly resembled his father."[89]

NEW MEDIUMS FOR PICASSO

During these postwar years, Picasso worked extensively in several different artistic mediums and styles. During the fall of 1945, he threw himself into lithography, which had been very popular in early-twentieth-century art circles and returned to popularity following World War II. He began working with a

talented printer, Fernand Mourlot, one of the best lithogra-
phers in Paris. One of the first lithographs that Picasso made
after the war (he had not done a single print since 1919) was a
portrait of a young girl, featuring a full view of her face.
Françoise Gilot had posed as his model. The following summer, while working in his studio in the Grimaldi Palace, he created a series of 11 lithographs (10 on June 14 and one the following day), all portraits of Françoise and no two alike. Like
his earlier lithograph of her, they all featured "the lovely oval of
her face and her gleaming eyes."[90] Today, the Grimaldi Palace
houses a museum dedicated to Picasso.

During the late 1940s, Picasso also revived his interest in
ceramics. In 1946, he met Georges and Suzanne Ramie, who
directed Madoura Ceramics, a factory in Vallauris, a small
town on the Côte d'Azur, which Picasso had first discovered
while out on a drive with a fellow artist in 1936. Picasso joined
the couple in their workshop, and he began to work in clay.

In 1948, he moved to Vallauris, living there with Françoise
and their son, Claude. He bought a house located on a hilltop
near the town. The site was known as the "Valley of Gold,"
because the soil there was quite rich. Picasso found the clay
nearby to be excellent for making pottery. For months, Picasso
enjoyed a happy life with Françoise and Claude. He would
work with clay in the Ramies' workshop during mornings,
then lunch with Françoise and Claude. Many afternoons, he
would go to the beach and take a swim.

Pottery remained a constant fascination for him, and, during this artistic phase, he produced 2,000 ceramic pieces in just
one year. He continued to work with ceramics for the rest of
his life. For Picasso, pottery combined several art forms into
one, including sculpture, drawing, and painting. He referred to
ceramics as sculpture without tears, because he could create a
small, finished work with a minimum of effort and labor.

In 1948, three years after the end of World War II, Picasso
still remained politically active. He became a devotee of
Communism and attended several World Peace Congresses,

which were Communist-sponsored. At a World Peace meeting held in Wroclaw, Poland, Picasso was invited to speak. The trip included his first flight in an airplane. He struggled with his speech, because he did not like public speaking. At the same time, despite his support for Communism, he came under attack by dissenters in the Soviet Union. His art was condemned, described by one Communist official as "a sickly apology for capitalist aesthetics."[91] Such accusations were generally lost on Picasso. In addition to attending the Congress, the aging Spanish artist also visited Auschwitz, the site of the most notorious Nazi death camp, which had a profound impact on him.

When another Communist Peace Congress was held in Paris in the spring of 1949, Picasso was again involved in controversy. A leader of the French Communist Party asked Picasso to design a poster for the planned event. The artist agreed. When Picasso did not produce the work, the Communist leader paid a call on the artist. Picasso had nothing ready for him and had no ideas. He had just finished work on a series of lithographs, though, which included one of a pigeon that Picasso's visitor took to be a dove, a symbol of peace. The fit was perfect, and the official left with Picasso's pigeon-turned-dove. Before the end of the day, "buildings of Paris were coated with reproductions of Picasso's pigeon announcing the Communist Peace Congress."[92] The posters immediately caused a firestorm of controversy that spread far beyond the streets of Paris. The lithograph was mocked, and his pigeon was changed in newspapers into a Soviet tank with feathers. Picasso refused to allow the controversy to affect him personally. As the Peace Congress met, Françoise gave birth to a girl, whom they called Paloma, Spanish for "dove."

Picasso's continuing support for the Communist Party would cause more controversy. In 1953, after the death of Joseph Stalin, he was asked to produce a portrait of the former Soviet Communist leader. He created a simple line drawing, which Françoise told Picasso looked exactly like a picture of her father. Picasso was amused. The Communists were not. They thought the portrait did not present Stalin in an appropriately heroic manner. Reporters arrived at Picasso's house and asked if "in doing the portrait of Stalin you wanted to make fun of him?"[93]

Despite these controversies, Picasso never renounced his membership in the Communist Party. His work with the party continued for many years. As the Cold War developed following World War II, he remained aligned with Communist ideology. During the Korean War (1950–1953), he painted a pair of murals, *War* and *Peace*, which condemned the U.S. government in the Korean conflict, depicting the United States as practicing germ warfare on its enemies, which never happened.

In 1956, Picasso became highly concerned when Russian tanks invaded Hungary, following protests concerning Soviet control of the Eastern European country. In a public act of defiance and criticism of Soviet policy in Eastern Europe, Picasso signed a letter calling for a special congress where Communist leaders could discuss the conflict between the Soviet Union and Hungary. During the 1950s, he opposed the U.S. government's trial of an American couple, Ethel and Julius Rosenberg, who were accused of spying for the Soviet Union and passing on atomic secrets. When he tried to attend a Communist peace conference in New York City, the U.S. State Department would not issue him a visa. For his support of Communism, Picasso received the Lenin Peace Prize twice, in 1952 and again in 1956.

During these years—the late 1940s and early 1950s—Picasso's relationship with Françoise slowly began to cool and he continued to have contact with his past loves. She discovered he was making visits every Thursday and Sunday to Marie-Therese. He spoke to her repeatedly of Marie-Therese and Dora Maar. Olga resurfaced and began following the couple around, on the streets and at the beach. Olga wrote letters to Picasso, which he read aloud to Françoise. In her memoirs,

Françoise wrote of her deteriorating relationship with Picasso:

> At the time I went to live with Pablo, I had felt that he was a person to whom I could, and should, devote myself entirely, but from whom I should expect to receive nothing beyond what he had given the world by means of his art. I consented to make my life with him on those terms ... During the next five or six years I had given my life over to him completely, I had had the children, and as a result of all that I was perhaps less capable of satisfying myself with such a Spartan attitude. I felt the need of more human warmth. And I thought that we had been working toward the point where such a thing was possible. Until some time after Paloma was born I continued to hope for that, and then gradually came to realize that I would get nothing more than what I had been willing to settle for at the beginning ... It took me a long time to work up to this realization, because I couldn't throw off all at once the hopes I had for something, since I had come to love him much more than I had loved him at the outset.[94]

Picasso had a reputation for treating his women gently—displaying love and affection—only to turn on them, becoming critical and verbally abusive. Eventually, he began seeing other women before breaking off these earlier relationships. Françoise was no exception. Toward the end of their long affair, "he eventually began to stay away from home for days at a time, then return to boast of escapades with new women."[95] By the early fall of 1953, she and her two children moved out of Picasso's house.

Picasso, however, had already moved on to other "new women." There was the writer Geneviève Laporte, with whom Picasso and Françoise had socialized earlier. He did not stay with her long, ending their relationship later in 1953. The elderly Picasso struggled with depression. His mental outlook was worsened when he received news of the death of his first wife,

In 1950, Picasso created *The Goat* from everyday items, such as ceramic pots, pieces of metal and wood, and a wicker basket, which he glued together with plaster. Picasso is pictured here in 1952 standing next to his sculpture in a gallery at the Salon De Mai in Paris.

Olga, as well as several of his artistic friends. He turned increasingly to solitude. In 1954, he went on a summer vacation to Perpignan, in southern France, where he finally recovered psychologically and emotionally. There, he spent long hours alone, on the beach and attending several bullfights.

His interest in ceramics continued through these turbulent years of domestic upheaval and change. He remained a regular in the Ramies' Vallauris workshop. He experimented with clay and free-form sculptures. He crafted works from discarded items, fashioning a piece titled *The Goat* (1950) out of everyday items, which were glued together with plaster. The following year he created *Baboon and Young*, which he made from a jug, a pair of toy cars, metal, and plaster. (The head and face of the baboon was formed by one of the cars, and marbles were used for the eyes.)

In the Ramies' pottery workshop, he met a sales clerk, Jacqueline Roque, the cousin of Suzanne Ramie. She soon became his new companion. The next woman in a long line of Picasso's lovers, it is believed "she was better able than any of his former women to adapt to his caprices and moods."[96] As he had done before when he took up with a new love, Picasso made another move. He relocated to a villa in Cannes, called *La Californie*, situated about five miles north of Vallauris. The mansion had been built around 1900 and was "ornately decorated with Art Nouveau stone carvings and wrought-iron grillwork."[97] It was there that he returned to his art, especially his painting.

To His
Last Day

Although his subjects always varied, Picasso spent his artistic talents painting several series of works, all variations of pieces by earlier European painters, such as Cranach, Velázquez, Courbet, David, El Greco, Delacroix, and the great impressionist painter Manet. He painted 15 versions of Delacroix's *Women of Algiers*. (In the final version, painted in 1955, he used Jacqueline Roque as the model for one of the figures.) Taking seventeenth-century Spanish painter Velázquez's famous work *Las Meninas* as his starting point, he spent two months creating 44 different versions of the 300-year-old painting. In one, he painted only in shades of blue. By reworking these older works of art, Picasso was, in a backhanded way, paying them tribute by recognizing their contribution to the history of art. At the same time, however, he was using this artwork as a springboard to recreate them in his own unique style. His series represents "at once a witty parody of Velázquez' masterpiece and a sober exploration of the ambiguities of art."[98]

In the late 1950s, Picasso created 44 variations of seventeenth-century Spanish artist Diego Velázquez's *Las Meninas* (The Maids of Honor). Pictured here is the fourteenth version of his *Las Meninas*, which is on display at the Museu Picasso in Barcelona.

THE WORLD AS HIS STAGE

With the arrival of the 1950s, Picasso was as popular and revered as ever. He seemed ageless, a painter in his 70s who rarely lacked the artistic energy to produce. The world was his stage, and art remained his continuing life's drama. On a personal level, however, Picasso's world was much smaller. He lived remotely, never traveling very far, making the southern coast of France his home. He almost never went abroad.

Friends came to him, to visit, to reminisce. It was an insular world, where Picasso ruled. In the book *The King of La Californie*, a Communist writer and friend described the "court life" of the aged Spanish artist:

> Picasso was the king. Everything and everybody revolves around him. His whim is law. No word of criticism is ever heard. There is a great deal of talk but very little serious discussion. Picasso behaves and is treated like a child who has to be protected. It is perfectly in order to like one picture better than another. But it is inconceivable that anybody should suggest that any painting is a total failure. There is no sense whatsoever of a struggle towards an aim: only a sense of Picasso struggling blindly within himself, and everybody else struggling to keep him amused and happy.[99]

Picasso's life had always followed a course set by his whims, both personal and artistic. Life at La Californie was no less whimsical, and, perhaps, even more so. The large house provided great, spacious rooms for his family and his many visitors; for his studio space, where he continued to produce his varied art projects; and for his burgeoning collection of artwork, some of which he had held onto for decades.

Throughout the house, rooms existed in chaos, cluttered with collections of objects he might want to use in a painting. His life had never been a neatly wrapped package. In his old age, more than ever, "disorder was a feature . . . where [Jacqueline], children, animals, friends, paintings, sculptures and souvenirs of all kinds combined to create an atmosphere buzzing with life, reflecting the artist's personality."[100] It was the world Picasso had made for himself, though, and he was happy.

Meanwhile, all around him, old friends were dying. His lifelong friend Paul Éluard died in 1952, followed in 1954 by the deaths of André Derain and Maurice Raynal, artistic comrades he had known since his days living in the Bateau-Lavoir. (Henri Matisse also died the same year.) Then, in 1955,

Fernand Léger passed away; he had been present, along with Braque, at the birth of cubism. As for Braque, he died in 1963. With these deaths and others, Paris lost some of its allure. It was in its streets, cafés, clubs, taverns, and studios, that Picasso and his artist friends had recreated the world of art.

Even as the art world of the late 1950s and early 1960s was embracing new forms and styles of art, including abstract expressionism and pop art, Picasso remained an icon. He was the subject of countless exhibitions and retrospectives, but he was still being offered commissions, especially for public works. In 1958, he completed a large mural for the Paris head-quarters of UNESCO, an agency of the United Nations.

Curious visitors, admirers, and tourists were a common annoyance outside his villa in Cannes. To escape from this unwanted scrutiny, Picasso moved again, this time to Vauvenargues, into an old and immense château in Provence, near Mont Sainte-Victoire, where the impressionist painter Cézanne had painted many of his works, some of which had been an inspiration for Picasso's early cubism. His new house was surrounded by nearly 2,000 acres of park-like lands, which kept unwanted visitors at a distance.

By the early 1960s, Picasso's life took yet another turn. He and Jacqueline would marry in May 1961, after he turned 80 years of age. The wedding was a small civil ceremony, with only two of their friends in attendance. With his new marriage, he moved yet again, this time to a country estate, "Notre Dame de Vie," in Mougins, just six miles from Cannes.

In 1965, the elderly Picasso became sick with an ulcer. He went to Paris for surgery. It would be his final visit to his beloved City of Light. His recovery from the operation was quite lengthy, and, for the rest of his life, he was impotent. This period in Picasso's life would be one of bitter experiences. The previous year, Françoise Gilot, who had finally left Picasso during the early 1950s, wrote and published a memoir of her years with the Spanish painter. Before its release, Picasso tried to block the book's publication.

(*continued on page 100*)

A CIRCLE OF FRIENDS

ARTISTIC COMPATRIOTS HELP TO INFLUENCE PICASSO'S WORK

Picasso's world was one filled with his creative, artistic genius, which often placed him at the center of his experiences. But it was also important to him to have good friends, close companions, and mutual artistic soul mates. Throughout his life, he cultivated friendships and lived in the midst of influential circles that were sometimes directed by him.

The pattern began at an early time in his artistic career. While attending the School of Fine Arts in Madrid, he made his first circle of friends who were fellow artists, including Manuel Pallares, Manuel Hugue, Sebastian Junyer-Vidal, and Carles Casagemas, "all of whom were to figure in his later life."* (Junyer-Vidal, for example, would accompany Picasso to Paris in 1904, when Pablo made the decision to move there permanently.)

While still a teenager living in Barcelona, he surrounded himself with a group of similarly young men who were part of the art world. Included in their number were Miguel Utrillo, who would become an important art historian; Ramon Casas, who emphasized the importance of "realism" in Picasso's art; and the enigmatic Post-Impressionist Henri de Toulouse-Lautrec. It was probably under Toulouse-Lautrec's influence that Picasso began experimenting with strong blocks of color and bold brush strokes. Utrillo helped stoke Picasso's appreciation of the late medieval Spanish painter El Greco. Such friendships, as well as others during this formative period, were crucial to the development of Picasso's art.

Others joined Picasso's circle. After his move to Paris in 1901, he met the art dealer Ambroise Vollard, who helped introduce the young Picasso at his first art shows and to critics and buyers. He also met the writer Max Jacob, who became a lifelong friend and colleague. He, too, had an impact on Picasso, generally by introducing him to other writers and poets, who became associates of the budding Spanish artist, including the poet and critic Guillaume Apollinaire and Alfred Jarry, a fellow bohemian and eccentric writer who defied all conventions and carried a pistol, a habit that young Picasso took up.

Often, such friendships gave Picasso the opportunity to make important contacts, including those who were wealthy patrons. Among his most important and influential patrons were the Steins, including Gertrude and her brother, Leo. Once they discovered Picasso and his works, they became buyers. They also introduced him into their circle of friends, which included some of the most important artists of the period, especially Henri Matisse. Picasso became a regular visitor to Gertrude Stein's apartment flat, where he met Matisse on a Saturday evening in 1906. Over time, they became friends on a professional basis.

When Picasso began to experiment with cubism, his close friends included fellow artists Georges Braque and Andre Derain, a leading fauvist whom Picasso convinced to experiment with cubism. He and Braque would become especially close, through their mutual dabbling with cubism. (At one point in their lives, they moved into houses next to one another.) The influence each had on the other was crucial. Other painters joined their cubist circle, including Juan Gris, a fellow Spanish painter, and Fernand Leger.

While many of Picasso's influential friends—artists, writers, art dealers, and patrons—came and went in his life, each had an impact on the great Spanish painter, both personally and professionally. One, perhaps, had the greatest impact of all. Picasso met Jaime Sabartés when the two were young and living in Paris in 1901. (Picasso painted a portrait of his new friend that year.) Although the two did not always live in close proximity—there would be times when Picasso still lived in Paris and Sabartés had returned to Spain—they remained good friends and confidants. Sabartés posed for various portraits for Picasso over the decades. No one would remain as constant a friend for Picasso throughout his life as Sabartés. Eventually, his friend would become his biographer.

Picasso's friendship meant a good deal to Jaime Sabartés, and he was determined to carry on Picasso's legacy. In 1963, a decade before Picasso's death, the city of Barcelona opened the Picasso Museum. It was Sabartés who had suggested to city officials to renovate a local medieval castle into a museum dedicated to his friend, Picasso, the greatest Spanish painter of the twentieth century. Sabartés personally spent three years on the project and donated more than 400 pieces of art to the museum from the private collection he had amassed over the years as one of Picasso's dearest friends.

* Lael Wertenbaker, *The World of Picasso, 1881–1973* (Amsterdam: Time-Life Books, 1984), 13.

(*continued from page 97*)
LIFE WITH PICASSO

In her book, *Life with Picasso*, Gilot described in stark detail the decade she had spent as Picasso's lover, companion, and mother of his children, Claude and Paloma. She described the artist as insensitive and demanding; self-absorbed and egotistical. She wrote of the great painter's excesses, tantrums, bullying, and vindictiveness, quoting Picasso, after their break-up: "I'd rather see a woman die, any day, than see her happy with someone else."[101] When Gilot informed Picasso of her intention to leave him, "in order to live with my own generation and

THE VALUE OF A PICASSO

Although Pablo Picasso lived long enough to become wealthy through his art, his paintings, sculptures, and other works did not always sell for top dollar. As a young artist, he sometimes struggled to sell any of his artwork. For years, he suffered financially, barely living hand to mouth. All that would change over the decades.

The decades sometimes moved slowly, however. When Picasso first encountered the art scene in Paris, he might have sold a painting for little more than the price of a meal. In 1900, the art collector Pedro Manach offered to pay Picasso 150 francs for all the art he produced each month. But this arrangement did not last, and Picasso spent the next few years in abject poverty.

Picasso persevered, his paintings were eventually noticed, and buyers began to appear. By 1912, in the midst of his cubist period, a London gallery sold Picasso works for amounts ranging between $10 and $100 each. This represented a significant increase, but Picasso's star was just beginning to rise. By the 1920s, the price for a Picasso painting went up considerably, and art collector Wilhelm Uhde was able to sell 13 of Picasso's paintings for 65,000 francs.

Following World War II, Picasso was one of the most famous artists in Europe, and museums, art galleries, and private collec-

the problems of my time,"[102] he acidly replied: "You imagine people will be interested in you? They won't ever, really, just for yourself. Even if you think people like you, it will only be a kind of curiosity they will have about a person whose life has touched mine so intimately. . . . For you, reality is finished; it ends right here. . . . If you attempt to take a step outside my reality . . . you're headed straight for the desert. And if you go, that's exactly what I wish for you."[103]

After Françoise ended her relationship with Picasso, he had all the things he had given her over the years—paintings,

tors around the world vied to purchase his works. By the 1960s, an important Picasso portrait sold in Great Britain for 32,000 pounds, followed by the sale of a cubist painting that brought an unheard of price of $500,000. In the years that followed, the sale of Picasso's works repeatedly shattered previous records for the amount paid for a single work of art.

In November 2000, a Picasso painting, *La Femme aux Bras Croises* (*Woman with Crossed Arms*), sold at auction for $55, million. Within four years, though, that record was completely shattered. In 2004, a 1905 painting, one from his Rose Period, sold at a Sotheby's auction for a whopping $104 million! (That price included the auction house's commission; the actual selling or auction "hammer" price was $93 million.) This price surpassed the previous record paid for a single work—$82.5 million paid in 1990 for Vincent Van Gogh's *Portrait of Doctor Gachet*.

Picasso's record-setting painting was a 99-year-old work, *Garçon à la Pipe* (*Boy with a Pipe*). The 2004 sale of the work was not the first time the painting had been sold. In 1950, John Whitney, a former U.S. ambassador to Great Britain, purchased *Garçon à la Pipe*, but Whitney did not pay anything near $100 million for the noted Picasso. His purchase price was $30,000, which today would be about $230,000, a fraction of that paid for the same work more than 50 years later.

drawings, personal objects, even private letters she had received from his friends, such as Matisse—removed from her house while she was on vacation in Venice. As a result of the publication of Gilot's scathing book, Picasso cut off all ties with his two children, Claude and Paloma. (As for the rest of Françoise Gilot's life, she went on to become a successful artist in her own right and eventually married Dr. Jonas Salk, developer of the polio vaccine. Today, she is in her 80s, and still works in her studios in Paris and New York.)

Despite the difficult situation with Gilot, Picasso tried to move on with his life. Since his physical problems continued, Picasso did not paint a single picture in 1966. That year, however, an old friend, André Malraux, who had become France's Minister of Cultural Affairs, helped organize a massive retrospective of Picasso. The exhibit was held in Paris for three months, and it included more than 1,000 of the Spanish artist's works, including paintings, sculptures, and graphics. Picasso did not remain inactive. Even in his final years, he was a vibrant force in modern art. In 1967, the city of Chicago purchased one of his most famous large sculptures, the enigmatic *Head of a Woman*.

CREATING UNTIL THE END

As he aged, Picasso sometimes became more, not less, productive, as if he had to continually prove himself in order to recreate his art. During one six-month period (March 16 through October 5, 1968), when the artist was 87 years old, he produced 347 drawings. (In the midst of this prolific artistic output, Picasso faced yet another tragic loss in his life, with the death of his longtime and loyal friend Jaime Sabartés.) Between 1969 and 1970, he produced at least 165 paintings, as well as many drawings. Sometimes, he produced paintings so fast that he dated them, not just by month and day, but with Roman numerals, indicating multiple works painted on the same day.

Generally, many of his later works, those produced during his last 10 or 20 years, are not perceived today as among his best. Some art critics describe Picasso as becoming lazy in his

In 1961, at the age of 80, Picasso married Jacqueline Roque, who was a sales clerk at Madoura Ceramics, which was owned by Picasso's friends, Georges and Suzanne Ramie. Picasso, who died in 1973, is pictured here with Jacqueline in the early 1970s.

art. Still others laud his output and its quality, believing his later works reveal how effortless artistic expression had become for Picasso.

In 1971, France's most imposing art institution, the Louvre, hosted an exhibit of Picasso's work, a rare singular tribute, given the museum does not generally honor artists who are still alive. The exhibit included eight of Picasso's works, placed on display in the museum's Grande Galerie.

Picasso continued to work as an artist until his last day. On April 8, 1973, Pablo Picasso, age 91, died of a heart attack at eleven in the morning, at his home at Notre Dame de Vie. Both his wife, Jacqueline, and his oldest son, who had been born to his Russian ballerina wife, Olga, were at his side when he died. The night before his death, he had been working on one more painting. He had been busy during the previous weeks preparing for a 200-piece exhibition of his artwork at an art museum in Avignon, in southeastern France.

Picasso was buried on the grounds of his estate, Château de Vauvenargues. As soon as his death was announced to the world, tributes began to pour in from everywhere. The sculptor Henry Moore lauded Picasso as the most gifted artist since the Italian Renaissance painter Raphael. French Minister of Cultural Affairs Maurice Druon praised the work of Picasso, stating the Spanish artist had "filled his century with his colours."[104]

At his death, Picasso left behind a world cluttered with broken relationships, illegitimate children, and a large private collection of artwork, both his and of other artists and friends, such as Braque, Cézanne, and Matisse. Since he left no will, the distribution of his estate had to be decided by the courts. In time, the legal battles ended with Picasso's wealthy art legacy, houses, and other properties being divided jointly between Jacqueline and all his children and grandchildren. The estate was worth tens of millions of dollars.

With his death, the modern art world mourned the passing of one of the most vibrant, prolific, innovative, and energetic artists of the twentieth century. No artist could lay claim to the sheer volume of Picasso's artistic productivity, which some experts estimate at 50,000 works, including paintings, sculpture, drawings, etchings, and ceramics. He had lived for so long and produced through so many decades that he was able to witness and make his own creative contributions to several genres of modern art.

What had driven the creative genius of Pablo Picasso? Art historians have struggled with this question both before and since his death. Perhaps it was his naturally rebellious human spirit; his driving nature that never allowed him to be satisfied with art that had already been created. He was a painter who never, even when his success as an artist was finally chiseled in stone, had a sense of having arrived, of having achieved an ultimate style of expression. This constant sense of adventure in approaching his art drove him relentlessly to reinvent his aesthetic view over and over again. One of Picasso's biographers, the art historian David Douglas Duncan, once recalled: "I had always wanted to know which was his favorite among all of the so-called "Periods" of his career—Blue . . . Rose . . . Cubist . . . Realist—which one? He was hugging Jacqueline, for she had just seen what he had done to her portrait. He looked up at me with his eyes really glowing and answered, 'The next one.'"[105]

How does one sum up Pablo Picasso's life? Perhaps to try is pointless. Perhaps Picasso himself would have considered such an effort frivolous. To this extraordinary and gifted Spanish artist, his art was not measured in the number of his works, but in having lived his life as he wanted, and to have taken his creative genius to the very edge of all that is defined as art. He had defined his life as his own and lived according to a philosophy that never allowed him to flinch or retreat. This is what made him Picasso. It was something he lived for—an abstract concept, a joy for life—that guided him through nine decades. Those close to him bear witness to his greatness and experienced his love affair with life. During their decade together, Françoise Gilot remembered a conversation she once had with the great artist:

> I told him if he had never painted a single picture in his life, we would probably have known of him as a philosopher. He laughed. "When I was a child, my mother said to me, 'If you become a soldier you'll be a general. If you become a monk you'll end up as the Pope.' Instead, I became a painter and wound up as Picasso."[106]

To become not only one of the greatest painters of the twentieth century, but to become *Picasso*—that was the diminutive Spaniard's ultimate success. He was an artist who never stopped, never flinched, never retreated, never regretted. In doing so, he challenged the entire world of art—past, present, and future.

Chronology and Timeline

1881   Pablo Picasso born on October 25, in Malaga, a small city in Spain's Andalusia region.

1891   Young Picasso's family moves to La Coruña, Spain.

1895   Family moves to Barcelona, where Picasso's father accepts a teaching position at the School of Fine Arts; Pablo enters the school as a young art student.

1896   Exhibits a painting at the National Exhibition of Fine Arts, in Madrid.

1897   Begins his studies at the Royal Academy of San Fernando, in Madrid.

1900   Visits Paris for the first time and soon makes the important art city his home.

1901   Under the influence of the great impressionists, Picasso is

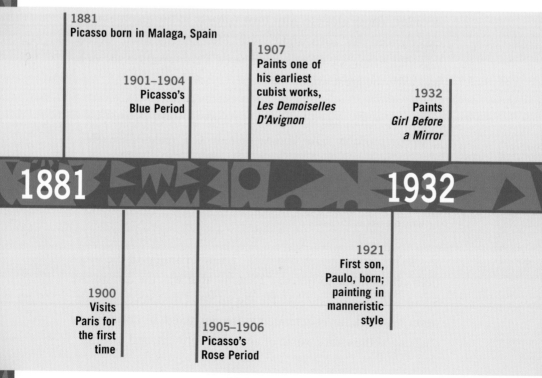

1881
Picasso born in Malaga, Spain

1901–1904
Picasso's
Blue Period

1907
Paints one of
his earliest
cubist works,
*Les Demoiselles
D'Avignon*

1932
Paints
*Girl Before
a Mirror*

1881   **1932**

1900
Visits
Paris for
the first
time

1905–1906
Picasso's
Rose Period

1921
First son,
Paulo, born;
painting in
manneristic
style

offered his first exhibition in Paris, at the gallery of Ambroise Vollard.

1901–04   During Picasso's Blue Period, he paints *Evocation* (1901), *The Absinthe Drinker* (1901), *The Old Guitarist* (1903), and *La Vie* (1903); he lives for a time in Barcelona.

1904   Moves back to Paris and lives in virtual poverty; he begins an eight-year relationship with Fernande Olivier.

1905–06   During Picasso's Rose Period, he paints the *The Acrobat Family* (1905), *Family of Saltimbanques* (1905), and *Boy Leading a Horse* (1905–1906); Gertrude Stein and her brother, Leo, begin buying Picasso's paintings; Picasso paints his famous portrait of Gertrude.

1906   The 24-year-old painter, at a turning point in his career, begins to experience a professional popularity; the Steins introduce him to Matisse; Picasso experiments with primitivism.

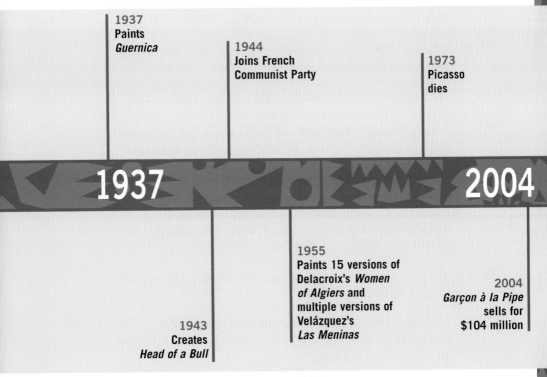

1937
Paints
Guernica

1944
Joins French
Communist Party

1973
Picasso
dies

1937   2004

1955
Paints 15 versions of
Delacroix's *Women
of Algiers* and
multiple versions of
Velázquez's
Las Meninas

2004
Garçon à la Pipe
sells for
$104 million

1943
Creates
Head of a Bull

1907	Paints one of his earliest cubist works, *Les Demoiselles D'Avignon*, "The Young Ladies of Avignon."
1909	Begins collaboration with Georges Braque—the two artists produce cubist works and share criticisms of one another's works; they collaborate until 1914.
1911	First public exhibition of Picasso's works in the United States takes place at the Photo Secession Gallery in New York.
1912	Fernande leaves Picasso—he soon begins a relationship with Marcelle Humbert; Picasso creates his three-dimensional cubist experiment, *Guitar*.
1914	World War I begins, taking several of Picasso's friends into military service; many never return.
1915–16	During the winter, Marcelle dies of tuberculosis.
1917	Begins working on scenery and costumes for Russian Ballet; he meets ballerina Olga Koklova.
1918	Marries Olga and moves into an apartment on an affluent street near the Champs-Elysées.
1921	Picasso is overjoyed at birth of his first son, Paulo; manneristic style paintings in this period include *Two Nude Women Seated* (1920) and *The Race* (1922), but his masterpiece of the early 1920s is a cubist work, *Three Musicians* (1921).
1925	Paints *The Three Dancers* in a pseudo-realist style that exaggerates human anatomy; other paintings in this style include *Woman in an Armchair* (1929), *Seated Bather* (1930), and *Figure in a Red Chair* (1932).
1927	Meets 17-year-old Marie-Therese Walter, and the two soon begin a secret affair.
1929	The Great Depression strikes, but Picasso is wealthy enough to weather the economic storm; he buys a château 40 miles outside of Paris.

1932	Paints one of his recognized masterpieces, *Girl Before a Mirror*.
1935	Olga leaves Picasso, and their marriage ends; Marie-Therese becomes pregnant.
1936	Marie-Therese gives birth to a daughter, Maya; Picasso provides the illustrations for a book of surrealist poetry; in Paris, three Picasso exhibits are held; that summer, Picasso meets Dora Maar, his next long-term companion.
1936–39	The Spanish Civil War pits the Republican government against Fascists, led by Francisco Franco.
1937	In January, Picasso agrees to paint a mural for the Spanish Government Pavilion at the Paris International Exhibition; in April, German pilots bomb the Basque city of Guernica, providing Picasso with the inspiration to paint *Guernica*—by July 12, the giant mural is on display in the Spanish Pavilion; later in the year, Picasso paints another cubist work, *Weeping Woman*.
1940	France is invaded and falls to Germany; Picasso is living in Paris, where he will remain until the war is over, five years later.
1940–44	Creates wartime art, including his famous *Head of a Bull* (1943), from a scrap bicycle's handlebars and seat; paints *Still Life with Ox Skull* (1942); turns 60 in 1941.
1943	Meets the painter Françoise Gilot, a woman in her early 20s—they are lovers for the next 10 years; at the same time, his relationship with Dora Maar is deteriorating. (Maar will go insane the following year.)
1944	Paris is liberated in August, ending Picasso's professional isolation; Picasso joins the French Communist Party in October; that fall, an exhibition of 70 of his paintings, called the "Salon de la Liberation," is held.
1944–45	Paints the black-and-white *Charnel House* after learning of Nazi concentration camps.

1947	Françoise gives birth to a boy whom they name Claude; during these years after World War II, Picasso experiments with lithography and ceramics even as he continues to paint.
1948	Attends and speaks at a world peace meeting held in Poland and sponsored by Communists.
1949	Françoise gives birth to a girl they name Paloma.
1950	Creates *The Goat*, a sculpture comprising discarded items.
1951	Creates *Baboon and Young*, another sculpture of scrap items, including a jug, a pair of toy cars, and metal and plaster.
1953	Creates a controversial lithograph featuring a portrait of Joseph Stalin and paints a pair of murals, *War* and *Peace*; Françoise leaves Picasso; his first wife, Olga, dies.
1954	Takes up with his new love, Jacqueline Roque.
1955	Paints 15 versions of Delacroix's *Women of Algiers*; paints multiple versions of Velázquez's *Las Meninas*.
1958	Completes a large mural for the Paris headquarters of UNESCO.
1961	At age 80, he marries Jacqueline.
1964	Former lover Françoise Gilot publishes a memoir of her years with Picasso and describes the Spanish painter as a difficult man with a violent temper—Picasso enraged by the publication of the book.
1965–66	Struggles with various illnesses, including an ulcer; does not paint a single work during 1966.
1967	The city of Chicago purchases a large Picasso sculpture, *Head of a Woman*.
1968–70	Engages in a flurry of painting, creating hundreds of canvases.

1971   The Louvre hosts a Picasso exhibition featuring eight of his works.

1973   Picasso dies of a heart attack at age 91.

2000   *La Femme aux Bras Croises* (Woman with Crossed Arms) is sold at auction for $55 million.

2004   *Garçon à la Pipe* (Boy with a Pipe) sells for $104 million.

Notes

Chapter 1

1 Morgan Gordan and Max Morgan, *Guernica: The Crucible of WWII* (New York: Witts, Stein, and Day, 1975), 258.
2 Herschel B. Chipp, *Picasso's Guernica* (Berkeley, Calif.: University of California Press, 1988), 31.
3 Lael Wertenbaker, *The World of Picasso, 1881–1973* (Amsterdam, The Netherlands: Time-Life Books, 1984), 126.
4 Andrew Brighton and Andrzej Klimowski, *Introducing Picasso* (New York: Totem, 1996), 136.

Chapter 2

5 Wertenbaker, *The World of Picasso*, 8.
6 Ibid., 9.
7 Brighton and Klimowski, *Introducing Picasso*, 9.
8 Stefano Loria, *Masters of Art: Pablo Picasso* (New York: Peter Bedrick, 1995), 6.
9 Wertenbaker, *The World of Picasso*, 9.
10 Ibid.
11 Ibid.
12 Ibid., 10.
13 Roland Penrose, *Picasso: His Life and Work* (New York: Harper, 1958), 25.
14 Ibid.
15 Wertenbaker, *The World of Picasso*, 10.
16 Ibid.
17 Penrose, *Picasso*, 29.
18 Wertenbaker, *The World of Picasso*, 11.
19 Ibid., 12.
20 Ibid., 14.
21 Ibid.
22 Ibid.
23 Ibid., 15.

Chapter 3

24 Ibid., 30.
25 Ibid.
26 Penrose, *Picasso*, 63.
27 Wertenbaker, *The World of Picasso*, 31.
28 Penrose, *Picasso*, 72.
29 Wertenbaker, *The World of Picasso*, 33.
30 Penrose, *Picasso*, 78.
31 Wertenbaker, *The World of Picasso*, 40.
32 Ibid., 43.
33 Loria, *Masters of Art*, 17.
34 Wertenbaker, *The World of Picasso*, 37.
35 Ibid.
36 Ibid., 38.
37 Ibid., 39.

Chapter 4

38 Ibid., 53.
39 Ibid.
40 Loria, *Masters of Art*, 20.
41 Wertenbaker, *The World of Picasso*, 54–55.
42 Brighton and Klimowski, *Introducing Picasso*, 44.
43 Penrose, *Picasso*, 126.
44 Brighton and Klimowski, *Introducing Picasso*, 42.
45 Wertenbaker, *The World of Picasso*, 61.
46 Ibid., 94.
47 Loria, *Masters of Art*, 28.
48 Penrose, *Picasso*, 149.
49 Ibid., 150.
50 Wertenbaker, *The World of Picasso*, 61.
51 Ibid.
52 Penrose, *Picasso*, 169.
53 Ibid.
54 Wertenbaker, *The World of Picasso*, 63.
55 Ibid.

Chapter 5

56 Penrose, *Picasso*, 187.
57 Wertenbaker, *The World of Picasso*, 73.
58 Penrose, *Picasso*, 188.
59 Ibid., 189.
60 Wertenbaker, *The World of Picasso*, 76.
61 Ibid., 79.
62 Ibid., 117.
63 Ibid., 100.
64 Ibid., 103.
65 Ibid., 118.
66 Ibid., 104.
67 Ibid., 108.
68 Ibid.
69 Ibid., 109.

Chapter 6

70 Ibid., 111.
71 Ibid., 125.
72 Ibid., 126.
73 Ibid.
74 Ibid., 127.
75 Ibid.
76 Maurice Raynal, *Picasso* (Cleveland, Ohio: World Publishing, 1969), 84.
77 John Berger, *The Success and Failure of Picasso* (Baltimore, Md.: Penguin, 1965), 166.
78 Wertenbaker, *The World of Picasso*, 127.
79 Penrose, *Picasso*, 312.
80 Ibid., 313.
81 Wertenbaker, *The World of Picasso*, 131.

Chapter 7

82 Ibid., 142.
83 Brighton and Klimowski, *Introducing Picasso*, 153.
84 Françoise Gilot and Carlton Lake, *Life with Picasso* (New York: McGraw-Hill, 1964), 13.
85 Ibid., 15.
86 Wertenbaker, *The World of Picasso*, 147.
87 Ibid.
88 Brighton and Klimowski, *Introducing Picasso*, 150.
89 Wertenbaker, *The World of Picasso*, 148.
90 Penrose, *Picasso*, 321.
91 Wertenbaker, *The World of Picasso*, 149.
92 Ibid.
93 Ibid., 151.
94 Gilot and Lake, *Life with Picasso*, 335.
95 Wertenbaker, *The World of Picasso*, 151.
96 Ibid.
97 Ibid., 152.

Chapter 8

98 Wertenbaker, *The World of Picasso*, 152.
99 Berger, *The Success and Failure of Picasso*, 180.
100 Loria, *Masters of Art*, 52.
101 Gilot and Lake, *Life with Picasso*, 351.
102 Ibid., 355.
103 Ibid.
104 "Art Master Picasso Dies": *http://news.bbc.co.uk/onthisday/hi/dates/stories/april/8/newsid_2523000/2523469.stm*
105 David Douglas Duncan, *The Private World of Pablo Picasso* (New York: Ridge Press, Harper, 1958), 158.
106 Gilot and Lake, *Life with Picasso*, 60.

Bibliography

Berger, John. *The Success and Failure of Picasso*. Baltimore, Md.: Penguin Books, 1965.

Brighton, Andrew, and Andrzej Klimowski. *Introducing Picasso*. New York: Totem, 1996.

Chipp, Herschel B. *Picasso's Guernica*. Berkeley, Calif.: University of California Press, 1988.

Duncan, David Douglas. *The Private World of Pablo Picasso*. New York: The Ridge Press, Harper, 1958.

Galloway, John. *Picasso*. New York: McGraw-Hill, 1969.

Gallwitz, Klaus. *Picasso: The Heroic Years*. New York: Abbeville, 1985.

Gilot, Françoise, and Carlton Lake. *Life with Picasso*. New York: McGraw-Hill, 1964.

Gordan, Morgan, and Max Morgan. *Guernica: The Crucible of WWII*. New York: Witts, Stein, and Day, 1975.

Heslewood, Juliet. *Introducing Picasso*. Boston, Mass.: Little, Brown, 1993.

Loria, Stefano. *Masters of Art: Pablo Picasso*. New York: Peter Bedrick, 1995.

Measham, Terry. *Picasso and His World*. Morristown, N.J.: Silver Burdett, 1980.

Padrta, Jiri, *Picasso: The Early Years*. New York: Tudor, 1961.

Penrose, Rolan. *Picasso: His Life and Work*. New York: Harper, 1958.

Raynal, Maurice. *Picasso*. Cleveland, Ohio: World, 1969.

Rubin, William, ed. *Picasso and Portraiture: Representation and Transformation*. New York: The Museum of Modern Art, Harry N. Abrams, 1996.

Wertenbaker, Lael. *The World of Picasso, 1881–1973*. Amsterdam: Time-Life Books, 1984.

Web sites

Picasso Archive
www.artchive.com/artchive/P/picasso.html

Information on Pablo Picasso
www.cyberspain.com/passion/picasso.htm

www.enchantedlearning.com/artists/Picasso

www.lucidcafe.com/library/95oct/ppicasso.html

Museum of Modern Art's Picasso Exhibition
www.moma.org/exhibitions/2003/MatissePicasso.html

Picasso Museum, Barcelona
www.museupicasso.bcn.es/eng/index_eng.html

Official Site of Pablo Picasso
www.picasso.fr/anglais/

Online Picasso Project, Texas A&M University
www.tamu.edu/mocl/picasso/

Further Reading

Beardsley, John. *Pablo Picasso*. New York: Harry N. Abrams, 1991.

Giraudy, Daniele, and Patrick De Maupeou. *Picasso and His Times*. New York: Henry Holt, 1999.

Meadows, Matthew. *Pablo Picasso*. New York: Sterling, 1996.

Muhlberger, Richard. *What Makes a Picasso a Picasso?* New York: Viking Children's Books, 1994.

Raboff, Ernest Lloyd. *Pablo Picasso*. New York: HarperCollins Children's Books, 1991.

Rollyson, Carl E. *Pablo Picasso*. Vero Beach, Fla.: Rourke Publishing, LLC, 1993.

Selfridge, John W. *Pablo Picasso*. Philadelphia, Pa.: Chelsea House, 1994.

Swisher, Clarice. *Pablo Picasso*. San Diego, Calif.: Lucent Books, 1995.

Index

Picture Credits

page:

9: © Associated Press, AP
11: © Associated Press, AP
14: © Giraudon/Art Resource, NY
21: © Giraudon/Art Resource, NY
35: © Erich Lessing/Art Resource, NY
40: © Scala/Art Resource, NY
45: © Time Life Pictures/Getty Images
48: © Bildarchiv Preussischer
      Kulturbesitz/Art Resource, NY

62: © Réunion des Musées Nationaux/Art
      Resource, NY
66: © Time Life Pictures/Getty Images
75: © John Bigelow Taylor/Art Resource, NY
78: © AFP/Gety Images
86: © Getty Images
92: © Getty Images
95: © Giraudon/Art Resource, NY
103: © CORBIS/SYGMA

Cover: © Getty Images

About the Author

Tim McNeese is Associate Professor of History at York College, in York, Nebraska. Professor McNeese earned an Associate of Arts degree from York College, a Bachelor of Arts in History and Political Science from Harding University, and a Master of Arts in History from Southwest Missouri State University.

A prolific author of books for elementary, middle and high school, and college readers, McNeese has published more than 70 books and educational materials over the past 20 years, on everything from Western wagon trains to the Space Race. His writing has earned him a citation in the library reference work *Something about the Author*. He recently appeared as a consulting historian for the History Channel series *Risk Takers, History Makers*. His wife, Beverly, is Assistant Professor of English at York College. They have two children, Noah and Summer. Readers are encouraged to contact Professor McNeese at tdmcneese@york.edu.